俺们

Our Good Times

山东小康之路影像纪实

A Collection of Photos of Shandong's Journey to General Prosperity

本书编写组 编
Edited by the Editing Group

山东省外事翻译中心 译
Translated by Shandong Provincial Translation and Interpretation Center

山东画报出版社

Shandong Pictorial Publishing House

编 委 会

俺们的小康

2020 年在新中国的历史上是极不平凡的一年。

这一年，脱贫攻坚取得全面胜利，决胜全面建成小康社会取得决定性成就。中国共产党领导全国各族人民，奋力拼搏，交出了一份载入史册的辉煌答卷。

从中国共产党的成立到中华人民共和国建立，从新中国的各项建设到改革开放、脱贫攻坚、全面建成小康社会，让全体中国人民过上幸福美好的生活一直是中国共产党执政的头等大事。一代又一代中国共产党人艰苦奋斗，砥砺前行，用一个个实践案例和一个个历史时间节点的辉煌成就，践行着自己的诺言。

通过珍贵而生动的照片和照片背后的故事来呈现小康社会建设的过程，叙述这一过程中闪烁的人与事，阅读视角独特而温暖。本书从数以万计的照片中筛选了 100 组，来展现山东人民小康社会建设的历程，用百姓的目光梳理小康社会建设的点点滴滴。照片和故事皆落脚于生活的细节和百姓的切身感受，通过一个个瞬间、一个个场景，朴素真实地反映时代的风貌及变迁，从中表达出百姓感受小康的细腻的家国情怀，让人读来亲切自然，感同身受。

"知屋漏者在宇下，知政失者在草野。"全面建成小康社会涉及教育、医疗、环境、住房、养老、交通等各个民生领域,人民群众对此最有发言权。小康社会的全面建成,最重要的标志就是全体人民过上幸福的生活。我们从一张张照片那发自肺腑的笑容中得到了答案。百姓的获得感、幸福感、安全感在他们的眼中,在他们的心里,真挚地流露出来。《俺们》,这个代表憨厚山东人的书名,和封面上的一个山村百姓纯朴的笑脸,最真实地表达了山东人民对小康生活的礼赞,代表着咱们山东老百姓过上好日子的兴高采烈和对生活的热爱。这是一种朴实无华的情感,也是全面建成小康社会成效最直观的体现。

中国共产党的百年奋斗史,就是为人民谋幸福的历史。站在"两个一百年"的历史交汇点,我们回顾过去,豪情满怀;憧憬未来,信心满满。我们期盼,在全面建设社会主义现代化国家的新征程中,百姓的小康日子会越过越红火!

Our Road to a Well-off Life

2020 was an extraordinary year in the history of the People's Republic of China.

It witnessed a complete victory in the fight against poverty, and decisive achievements in securing a full victory in building a moderately prosperous society in all respects. The Communist Party of China led the Chinese people of all ethnic groups in forging ahead, and scored historic achievements.

From the founding of the CPC, the founding of the People's Republic of China, and the various endeavors of new China, to reform and opening-up, the fight against poverty and completing the building of a moderately prosperous society, creating a better life for all the Chinese people has always been the top priority of the CPC. The CPC members, generation over generation, have worked hard to press ahead and practice their promises with concrete actions and fruitful results.

It is a unique and warm perspective to present the journey to general prosperity through valuable and lively images and the stories behind. This book selects 100 photos from tens of thousands of photos to show the process of building a moderately prosperous society in Shandong, and sorts out the bits and pieces of those years from the perspective of the people. All the photos and stories tell the details of people's daily life. Through moments and scenes, they vividly reflect the changes of the times, express people's love for their hometowns and the country, and strike a chord with readers.

As an old Chinese saying goes, "One who lives under the roof knows it when it leaks; one who lives among the folk knows it when the government policy is wrong". Building a moderately prosperous society in all respects involves education, medical care, environment, housing, elderly care, transportation and other fields of people's livelihood. Thus, the people have the most say in this. The most important hallmark of completing this process is a well-off life for all the people. From the genuine smiles on the photos, we can find the fruit of all the efforts. From people's eyes, we can feel their sense of fulfillment, happiness and security. The title of this book, which is simple and direct as the people of Shandong, as well as the genuine smiles on the cover, expresses Shandong people's satisfaction with the happy life now. This sentiment, maybe simple and unadorned, speaks volume about the effects of fully building a moderately prosperous society.

The CPC's endeavor over the past 100 years is to pursue happiness for the people. At a historical stage where the timeframes of its two centenary goals converge, we feel boundless pride when reviewing the past, and are full of confidence when looking ahead. As we embark on a new journey of fully building a modern socialist country, we look forward to an even more thriving life.

综　述

　　小康社会是中华民族自古以来追求的理想社会状态。使用"小康"这个概念来确立中国的发展目标，既符合中国发展实际，也深得人民的理解和支持。我们党提出，到建党一百年时建成经济更加发展、民主更加健全、科教更加进步、文化更加繁荣、社会更加和谐、人民生活更加殷实的小康社会，然后再奋斗三十年，到新中国成立一百年时，把我国建成社会主义现代化国家。全面建成小康社会、实现第一个百年奋斗目标之后，我国开启了社会主义现代化建设新征程，向第二个百年奋斗目标进军。

　　小康社会建设是我国社会主义现代化进程中具有里程碑意义的重要阶段。新中国成立以来，我们党团结带领全国各族人民一直为过上幸福美好的生活而努力奋斗。从建国初期改变一穷二白面貌到建设社会主义现代化、从小康社会建设到总体小康、全面小康，从决战决胜全面建成小康社会，到全面建成小康社会宏伟蓝图变成现实，一以贯之的主题，就是把我国建设成为社会主义现代化国家。这一实践路径，使人民群众的获得感、幸福感、安全感不断增强，推动着现代化建设从量的积累到质的飞跃。体现了我们党不忘初心，始终把为人民谋幸福、为民族谋复兴作为自己的使命；体现了与时俱进，始终把人民过上更加美好生活的新期待作为努力方向。

一、从"小康之家"到"全面建成小康社会"的历史演进

"小康"是中国古代思想史上反映中华民族向往和追求幸福的一个概念，最早出现在距今2500年的《诗经·大雅》之中："民亦劳止，汔可小康"。意思是要轻徭薄赋、与民休息，让老百姓过上小康安乐的日子。《礼记·礼运》中讲到两种社会模式，有"天下为公"的"大同"和"天下为家"的"小康"。其中的"小康"指介于温饱和富裕之间的生活状态，是作为理想社会最高形态大同社会的初级形式。

尽管不同时代的小康所承载的内容有所不同，但都表达了人们对美好生活的向往。"小康"不仅是中国人自古以来的梦想，也是中国共产党带领中华民族走向复兴的阶段性目标。

1. 提出"小康之家"

在中国共产党历史上，提出"小康"和推进四个现代化建设直接相关。1979年12月6日，邓小平同志接见日本首相大平正芳时说道："我们要实现的四个现代化，是中国式的四个现代化，是'小康之家'。"这是我党第一次用小康来描述中国的发展前景，也是第一次用"小康"代替之前"四

个现代化"的提法。从此，小康社会建设作为我党的奋斗目标伴随了改革开放进程，呈现出不同的阶段性发展特征。

2. 提出并实施"三步走"经济发展战略

1987 年 4 月 30 日，邓小平同志在同西班牙政府副首相格拉的会谈中第一次完整描绘了"三步走"经济发展战略。1987 年 10 月 25 日，"三步走"经济发展战略在党的十三大报告中以党的奋斗目标得以阐述："党的十一届三中全会以后，我国经济建设的战略部署大体分三步走。第一步，实现国民生产总值比一九八〇年翻一番，解决人民的温饱问题。这个任务已经基本实现。第二步，到本世纪末，使国民生产总值再增长一倍，人民生活达到小康水平。第三步，到下个世纪中叶，人均国民生产总值达到中等发达国家水平，人民生活比较富裕，基本实现现代化。然后，在这个基础上继续前进。"〔《沿着有中国特色的社会主义道路前进——在中国共产党第十三次全国代表大会上的报告》，人民出版社 1987 年 11 月版。〕在这个宏伟战略安排中，小康目标被列为"三步走"中的第二步，由此成为我国现代化进程中的一个重要阶段。

3. "小康"的经济标准扩展为衡量社会全面进步的标准

1991 年 3 月，《关于国民经济和社会发展十年规划和第八个五年计划纲要的报告》指出："我们所说的小康生活，是适应我国生产力发展水平，体现社会主义基本原则的。人民生活的提高，既包括物质生活的改善，也包括精神生活的充实；既包括居民个人消费水平的提高，也包括社会福利和劳动环境的改善。"可见，这时的"小康"不仅是衡量经济发展、人民生活水平的标准，还是衡量社会全面进步的标准。

经过 20 世纪 80 年代和 90 年代二十年的努力奋斗，"三步走"战略中的前两步目标顺利实现，完成了从"温饱"到"小康"的跨越。

4. 从"总体上达到小康"转向"全面建设小康社会"

1997 年 9 月，党的十五大报告中把"三步走"战略中的第三步细分三个阶段性目标，形成了一个新的"三步走"战略："第一个十年实现国民生产总值比二〇〇〇年翻一番，使人民的小康生活更加宽裕，形成比较完善的社会主义市场经济体制；再经过十年的努力，到建党一百年时，使国民经济更加发展，各项制度更加完善；到世纪中叶建国一百年时，基本实现现代化，建成富强民主文明的社会主义国家。"〔《十五大以来重要文献选编》（上），《高举邓小平理论伟大旗帜，把建设有中国特色社会主义事业全面推向二十一世纪》，人民出版社2000年6月版，第4页。]

党的十五届五中全会进一步提出，我国将从新世纪开始"进入和建设小康社会的新发展阶段"。

2001年7月，建党八十周年纪念大会宣告："十二亿中国人不仅解决了温饱问题，而且总体上达到小康水平。"这标志着我国目标已由总体小康转向了全面小康。

5. 从全面建设小康社会到"全面建成小康社会"

2002年，党的十六大报告中指出："现在达到的小康还是低水平的、不全面的、发展很不平衡的小康。"要在21世纪头二十年，集中力量，全面建设惠及十几亿人口的更高水平的小康社会。

党的十七大报告进一步发展了小康社会的内涵，对全面建设小康社会提出了新的更高要求。比如，强调转变发展方式、实现经济"又好又快"发展，"扩大社会主义民主""加强文化建设""加快发展社会事业""建设生态文明"等内容，更加突出全面建设小康社会的阶段性和以人为本的理念。

　　2012 年 11 月 8 日，党的十八大报告中首次把"全面建设小康社会"上升为"全面建成小康社会"，提出了一系列新思想、新论断、新要求，小康社会建设进入到全面建成的决定性阶段。习近平总书记指出："党的十八大……对全面建设小康社会目标进行了充实和完善，提出了更具明确政策导向、更加针对发展难题、更好顺应人民意愿的新要求。这些目标要求，与党的十六大提出的全面建设小康社会奋斗目标和党的十七大提出的实现全面建设小康社会奋斗目标新要求相衔接，也与中国特色社会主义事业总体布局相一致"。

6. 决战决胜全面建成小康社会

　　2017 年党的十九大到 2020 年 12 月，全面建成小康社会进入决胜期，进而开启全面建设社会主义现代化国家新征程。这一阶段的实践突出打好打赢三大攻坚战，尤其是精准脱贫攻坚战。

　　习近平总书记在党的十九大报告中提出："到建党一百年时建成经济更加发展、民主更加健全、科教更加进步、文化更加繁荣、社会更加和谐、人民生活更加殷实的小康社会，然后再奋斗三十年，到新中国成立一百年时，基本实现现代化，把我国建成社会主义现代化国家"。

7. 全面建成小康社会转向全面建设社会主义现代化国家

党的十九届五中全会明确指出："'十四五'时期是我国全面建成小康社会、实现第一个百年奋斗目标之后，乘势而上开启全面建设社会主义现代化国家新征程、向第二个百年奋斗目标进军的第一个五年。"我国进入新发展阶段。党的十九届五中全会描绘了我国进入新发展阶段的发展蓝图，擘画了全面建设社会主义现代化国家的宏伟愿景。这是我国在新时代接续努力，向第二个百年奋斗目标进军的行动纲领。

上述历史演进表明，从邓小平同志提出"小康之家"，到实施"三步走"战略，实现从"温饱"到"小康"，再由总体小康转向全面小康，直至党的十八大以来进入全面建成小康社会的决定性阶段，2020 年实现全面建成小康社会目标，小康社会目标一直伴随着 40 多年的改革开放进程。这一实践路径，体现了我党追求奋斗目标的历史延续性和阶段性发展特征，推动着小康社会建设从总体到全面、从低水平到高水平、从量的积累到质的飞跃。

二、全面建成小康社会重要论述蕴含新发展

党的十八大以来，习近平总书记关于全面建成小康社会有诸多重要论

述，内容十分丰富。仅《习近平关于全面建成小康社会论述摘编》一书就收录了从 2012 年 11 月 15 日至 2016 年 3 月 10 日习总书记的讲话、谈话、演讲、贺信、指示等 332 个自然段的内容。习近平总书记关于全面建成小康社会的大量论述，散见于各种场合。有在国际场合，向国际社会介绍全面建成小康社会的目标；有用群众语言描述全面建成小康社会的愿景；有针对现实分析全面建成小康社会的重点和难点；也有从满足人民需要出发，对全面建成小康社会内涵进行的丰富和拓展；还有对全面建成小康社会在我国经济社会发展中新定位的论述。这些重要论述蕴含着诸多创新，赋予全面建成小康社会新的丰富内涵，体现了对我党以往奋斗目标的继承、丰富和发展，凸显了与时俱进的时代特征。

1. 刻画了新坐标：实现"中国梦"的关键一步

实现中华民族伟大复兴，是近代以来中华民族最伟大的梦想。在我们党的文献中，"实现中华民族伟大复兴"最早是在党的十三大报告中提出的。2013 年 3 月 17 日，习近平总书记在第十二届全国人民代表大会第一次会议上的讲话："实现全面建成小康社会、建成富强民主文明和谐的社会主义现代化国家的奋斗目标，实现中华民族伟大复兴的中国梦，就是要实现国家富强、民族振兴、人民幸福，既深深体现了今天中国人的理想，也深深反映了我们先人们不懈追求进步的光荣传统。"从而把全面建成小康社会和实现中国梦紧密联系起来。

2013 年 4 月 28 日，习近平总书记在同全国劳动模范代表座谈时，从实现中国梦的角度阐述了全面建成小康社会问题："我们已经确定了今后的奋斗目标，这就是到中国共产党成立 100 年时全面建成小康社会，到新中国成立 100 年时建成富强民主文明和谐的社会主义现代化国家，努力实现中华民族伟大复兴的中国梦。"

这些论述进一步丰富和发展了伟大梦想的当代内涵、实现路径和实践要求。

2. 概括了新特征：覆盖人群全、涉及领域全

习近平总书记多次论述"全面"，认为这个"全面"，体现在覆盖的人群是全面的，是"不分地域"的小康，是"不让一个人掉队"的小康。这个"全面"，体现在所涉及的五大建设领域也是全面的。2012 年 12 月 29 日，习近平总书记到河北阜平看望慰问困难群众时说："全面建成小康社会，最艰巨最繁重的任务在农村、特别是在贫困地区。没有农村的小康，

特别是没有贫困地区的小康，就没有全面建成小康社会。"〔《在河北省阜平县考察扶贫开发工作时的讲话》，中央文献出版社2015年版，第16页。〕2015年1月20日，习近平总书记在昆明会见怒江州贡山独龙族怒族自治县干部群众代表时强调："全面实现小康，一个民族都不能少！""我们实现第一个百年奋斗目标、全面建成小康社会，没有老区的全面小康，特别是没有老区贫困人口脱贫致富，那是不完整的。这就是我常说的小康不小康、关键看老乡的涵义。"〔《把革命老区发展时刻放在心上——习近平总书记主持召开陕甘宁革命老区脱贫致富座谈会侧记》〕2015年10月16日，习近平出席减贫与发展高层论坛，提出"全面小康是全体中国人民的小康，不能出现有人掉队"。

全面建成小康社会覆盖的领域也是全的。2013年3月27日，习近平在金砖国家领导人第五次会晤时指出："面向未来，中国将相继朝着两个宏伟目标前进：一是到2020年国内生产总值和城乡居民人均收入比2010年翻一番，全面建成惠及十几亿人口的小康社会。二是到2049年新中国成立100年时建成富强民主文明和谐的社会主义现代化国家。我们将坚持以人为本，全面推进经济建设、政治建设、文化建设、社会建设、生态文明建设，促进现代化建设各个方面、各个环节相协调，建设美丽中国。"

全面建成小康社会是"干部清正、政府清廉、政治清明""找到全社会意愿和要求的最大公约数""国家物质力量和精神力量都增强，全国各族人民物质生活和精神生活都改善"的小康，是"让人民群众在每一个司法案件中都感受到公平正义"的小康，是"望得见山、看得见水、记得住乡愁"的全面小康，是"为实现中国梦提供坚强力量支撑"的全面小康。全面建成小康社会覆盖到了五大建设领域。

3. 揭示了本质：根本上说是"发展问题"

习近平总书记多次论述发展问题，揭示了全面建成小康社会的本质是发展。2014 年 1 月 1 日，习近平总书记发表讲话："全面建成小康社会，实现社会主义现代化，实现中华民族伟大复兴，最根本最紧迫的任务还是进一步解放和发展社会生产力。解放思想，解放和增强社会活力，是为了更好解放和发展社会生产力。……我们要通过深化改革，让一切劳动、知识、技术、管理、资本等要素的活力竞相迸发，让一切创造社会财富的源泉充分涌流。"［习近平：《切实把思想统一到党的十八届三中全会精神上来》，《求是》2014 年 01 期］2014 年 7 月 16 日，习近平在巴西国会的演讲中指出："当前，中国人民正在为实现中华民族伟大复兴的中国梦而奋斗。中国是世界上最大的发展中国家，发展是解决中国所有问题的关键。"

全面建成小康社会的本质在党的十九大报告中也被提及：我国社会主要矛盾的变化，没有改变我们对我国社会主义所处历史阶段的判断，我国仍处于并将长期处于社会主义初级阶段的基本国情没有变，我国是世界最大发展中国家的国际地位没有变。"三个没有变"揭示了当代中国国情的本质特征，决定了我们的根本任务是集中力量发展社会生产力，发展是解决中国所有问题的关键。

我国一直在实现发展，但发展的主题在转换。从纵向来看，1978 年至 1997 年，主要解决"不发展"问题，即贫穷落后的问题。1997 年至 2012 年党的十八大召开，主要解决"发展中"的问题。党的十八大以来主要解决发展起来以后所面临的问题。当下，我国经济已由高速增长转向高质量发展。这就要求提高全要素生产率，在追求高质量高效益中实现全面建成小康社会的目标。

4. 对内涵进行了新拓展：涵盖到人民身体健康

2013 年 8 月 31 日，习近平总书记会见参加全国群众体育先进单位和先进个人表彰会、全国体育系统先进集体和先进工作者表彰会的代表时指出：“全民健身是全体人民增强体魄、健康生活的基础和保障，人民身体健康是全面建成小康社会的重要内涵，是每一个人成长和实现幸福生活的重要基础。”2014 年 12 月 13 日，习近平总书记在江苏镇江市丹徒区世业镇卫生院调研，了解农村医疗卫生事业发展和村民看病就医情况，同前来就诊的农民交谈时指出：“没有全民健康，就没有全面小康。”这些论述已把我党的奋斗目标和每个家庭、每个人的成长、生活紧紧联系在一起。

2020 年发生新冠肺炎疫情，习近平总书记牵挂着人民群众生命安全和身体健康，作出一系列批示，多次发表讲话。强调：我们始终坚持把人民群众生命安全和身体健康放在第一位。采取切实有效措施，坚决遏制疫情蔓延势头。习近平总书记指出：“确保人民群众生命安全和身体健康，是我们党治国理政的一项重大任务。”〔《习近平主持召开中央全面深化改革委员会第十二次会议时的讲话》〕这些重要论述，不仅丰富拓展了全面建成小康社会的内涵，而且把确保人民身体健康上升到治国理政的高度。

5. 论述了全面建成小康社会在“四个全面”战略布局中的目标定位

“四个全面”战略布局是一个有机联系的整体，具有鲜明的系统性和战略性。全面建成小康社会、全面深化改革、全面依法治国、全面从严治党不是并列关系，全面深化改革、全面依法治国、全面从严治党都是手段，而全面建成小康社会则是目标，是"处于引领地位的战略目标"。只有全面深化改革，破除利益藩篱，实现全面建成小康社会才有动力；只有全面依法治国，建立规则秩序，推进公平正义，实现全面建成小康才有保障；只有全面从严治党，锻造领导核心，提供政治支撑，实现全面建成小康才有保证。

党的十九届五中全会把"四个全面"战略布局中的"全面建成小康社会"发展为"全面建设社会主义现代化国家"，将两个一百年奋斗目标有机衔接。

三、开启全面建设社会主义现代化国家新征程

全面建成小康社会是我国社会主义现代化进程中的一个阶段性目标。党的十九大报告指出："从十九大到二十大，是'两个一百年'奋斗目标的历史交汇期。我们既要全面建成小康社会、实现第一个百年奋斗目标，又要乘势而上开启全面建设社会主义现代化国家新征程，向第二个百年奋斗目标进军。"表明，全面建成小康社会是开启全面建设社会主义现代化国家新征程的起点，具有承上启下的地位作用。

党的十九大报告指出："从 2020 年到 2035 年，在全面建成小康社会的基础上，再奋斗十五年，基本实现社会主义现代化。从 2035 年到本世纪中叶，在基本实现现代化的基础上，再奋斗十五年，把我国建成富强民主文明和谐美丽的社会主义现代化强国。" 可见，全面建成小康社会这个新起点，地位重要，影响深远，是我国社会主义现代化建设中的里程碑。

实现全面建成小康社会，完成了消除绝对贫困的艰巨任务，这是永载史册的伟大功绩，开启了波澜壮阔的豪迈征程。这是中国人民的伟大光荣，是中国共产党的伟大光荣，是中华民族的伟大光荣！奋斗百年，中国共产党人咬定青山，不忘初心，坚韧不拔，接续奋斗。全面建成小康社会不是终点，而是新生活、新奋斗的起点。

2021 年，进入"十四五"时期，起航社会主义现代化国家建设新征程，我国也进入新发展阶段。新发展阶段，就是全面建设社会主义现代化国家向第二个百年奋斗目标进军的阶段。关于这个新发展阶段，2021 年 1 月 11 日，习近平总书记在中央党校省部级主要领导干部专题研讨班上的重要讲话指出："新发展阶段是社会主义初级阶段中的一个阶段，同时是其中经过几十年积累、站到了新的起点上的一个阶段。新发展阶段是我们党带领人民迎来从站起来、富起来到强起来历史性跨越的新阶段。新发展阶段是我国社会主义发展进程中的一个重要阶段。社会主义初级阶段不是一个静态、一成不变、停滞不前的阶段，也不是一个自发、被动、不用费多大气力自然而然就可以跨过的阶段，而是一个动态、积极有为、始终洋溢着蓬勃生机活力的过程，是一个阶梯式递进、不断发展进步、日益接近质的飞跃的量的积累和发展变化的过程。"

2021 年，是"十四五"开局之年，开好局起好步至关重要。习近平总书记强调，从全面建成小康社会到基本实现现代化，再到全面建成社会主义现代化强国，是新时代中国特色社会主义发展的战略安排。我们要坚韧不拔、锲而不舍，以昂扬姿态奋力开启全面建设社会主义现代化国家新征程，奋力谱写社会主义现代化新征程的壮丽篇章。

Overview

A moderately prosperous society has been an ideal state of society pursued by the Chinese nation since ancient times. Identifying "moderate prosperity" as a development goal not only conforms to China's reality, but also wins broad understanding and support among the people. Our Party has developed the vision that, by the time we celebrate our centenary, we will have developed our society into a moderately prosperous one with a stronger economy, greater democracy, more advanced science and education, thriving culture, greater social harmony, and a better quality of life. After this, with another 30 years of work, and by the time we celebrate the centenary of the People's Republic of China, we will have turned China into a modern socialist country. After finishing building a moderately prosperous society in all respects and achieving the first centenary goal, we now embark on a new journey toward the second centenary goal of fully building a modern socialist country.

Building a moderately prosperous society is a milestone in China's modernization efforts. Since the founding of New China, the Party has united and led all the Chinese people in pursuit of a better life. From being an impoverished country in its nascent years, China has achieved the goal of becoming a moderately prosperous society in all respects. Building a modern socialist country has been an overarching theme during this process. These practices have increased people's sense of benefit, happiness and security, and facilitated the qualitative change of modernization on the basis of quantitative increase. It also shows that the CPC remains true to its original aspiration, works for happiness of the people and rejuvenation of the nation, keeps pace with the times, and always strives to meet people's new expectations for a better life.

I. The evolution from a "Xiaokang Society" to a "Moderately Prosperous Society in All Respects"

It has been the Chinese people's wish since ancient times to live a life of Xiaokang, namely a life of peace, stability and happiness. The term was first seen in *The Book of Songs · Major Odes*, saying that ordinary people have toiled too much, and they need to live a life of Xiaokang. It means reducing the burden of taxation and giving people time to rest, so that they can lead a comfortable and happy life. *The Book of Rites · Conveyance of Rites* wrote about two social models. One emphasizes the pursuit of the common good, and the other one is Xiaokang, which refers to a status of moderate prosperity in which people are neither too rich nor poor but free from want and toil. This is the initial stage of the harmonious society, which is the ultimate phase of an ideal society.

The content of Xiaokang in different eras may be different, but they all reflect people's yearning for a better life. Xiaokang has not only been the dream of the Chinese since ancient times, but also a goal for the current stage on the path towards rejuvenation of the Chinese nation led by the CPC.

1. The vision of a Xiaokang Society

In the history of the CPC, the inception of Xiaokang is directly connected with the Four Modernizations. When meeting with Masayoshi Ohira, Prime Minister of Japan, on December 6, 1979, Deng Xiaoping said that the Four Modernizations we hoped to achieve were a Xiaokang society with Chinese style. This was the first time that our Party had used the word Xiaokang to describe China's development prospects, and it was also the first time that "Xiaokang Society" was used to replace the previous term "Four Modernizations". Since then, Xiaokang society, as the Party's goal, has been integrated with the reform and opening-up process, showing different characteristics on different stages.

2. Three-step strategy for economic development

The three-step strategy for economic development was first put forward in a systemic way by Deng Xiaoping during his meeting with Alfonso Guerra, Deputy Prime Minister of Spain, on April 30, 1987. On October 25, 1987, the three-step economic development strategy was stated in the report to the 13th National Congress of the CPC, "After the Third Plenary Session of the Eleventh CPC Central Committee, the economic development of our country will be roughly divided into 3 steps. First, double the GDP on the basis of that of 1980 to ensure that people's basic needs are met. This goal has basically been achieved. Second, double the GDP again by the end of this century and make sure that people's lives are generally decent. Third, by the middle of the next century, the per capita GDP will reach the level of moderately developed countries, and the people will have a better quality of life, and modernization will be basically achieved. Then, we will strive for more progress on this basis." (*Advancing along the Road of Socialism with Chinese Characteristics—Report to the 13th National Congress of the CPC*, People's Publishing House, November 1987) In this grand strategic arrangement, the goal of moderate prosperity was listed as the second step in the "three-step" strategy, thus becoming an important stage in our country's modernization process.

3. Moderate prosperity expanded from a standard measuring economic development to the one measuring social progresses in all respects

In March 1991, the *Report for the Ten-Year Plan and the 8th Five-Year Plan for Economic and Social Development* elaborated that, "The moderately prosperous society should be in line with the development level of our country's productive force, and reflect the basic principles of socialism. It should enable people not only to enjoy a better life in material terms, but also to live a more enriching intellectual and cultural life. It includes not only higher individual consumption level of residentes, but also better social welfare and working environment." Therefore, moderate prosperity is not only a standard measuring economic development and people's living conditions, but also one for the overall progress of the society.

After two decades of hard work in the 1980s and 1990s, the first two goals of the three-step strategy have been successfully achieved, and a leap has been made from subsistence to initial prosperity.

4. Transformation from initial prosperity to a moderately prosperous society in all respects

In September 1997, the report to the 15th National Congress of the CPC further divided the third part of the three-step strategy into 3 goals based on different stages. "In the first ten years, the GDP will be doubled compared with that in 2000, so that people will lead a more prosperous life, and a relatively complete socialist market economy system will be formed. With another ten years, by the time the Party celebrates its centenary, the economy will be more developed and institutions in all fields will be further improved. By the time we celebrate the centenary of the People's Republic of China, we will have basically achieved modernization and turned China into a modern socialist country that is prosperous, strong, democratic and culturally advanced. [*Selection of Important*

Literature since the 15th National Congress of the CPC, (*Volume One*), *Uphold the Banner of Deng Xiaoping Theory and Bring the Socialism with Chinese Characteristics into the 21st Century*, People's Publishing House, June 2000, page 4]

The 5th Plenary Session of the 15th CPC Central Committee put forward the vision that the start of the new century would mark "a new stage for building a moderately prosperous society".

In July 2001, the meeting marking the 80th anniversary of the CPC announced that, "The basic needs for 1.2 billion people have been met, and their lives are generally decent." This marked that China's goal had shifted from initial prosperity to moderate prosperity in all respects.

5. From building a moderately prosperous society in all respects to finishing the building of a moderately prosperous society in all respects

As stated in the report to the 16th National Congress of the CPC in 2002, "The well-off life we are leading now is still at a low level; It is not all-inclusive and is very uneven." China would concentrate on building a higher level of well-off society that benefits over 1 billion population in the first two decades of the 21 century.

The report to the 17th National Congress of the CPC further developed the connotation of moderate prosperity, and raisted the standards for fully building a moderately prosperous society in all respects. For example, emphasis was put on transforming the mode of development, promoting the sound and rapid development of economy, expanding socialist democracy, promoting cultural development, accelerating the development of social programs and building ecological civilization. Among others, the people-centered philosophy and the new phase of fully building a moderately prosperous society in all respects were highlighted.

The report to the 18th National Congress of the CPC held on November 8, 2012, upgraded from "building a moderately prosperous society in all respects" to "finishing the building of a moderately prosperous society in all respects" for the first time. New thinking, new judgments and new requirements from the report brought the building of a moderately prosperous society into a decisive stage. General Secretary Xi Jinping pointed out that the 18th National

Congress of the CPC enriched and improved the goal of building a moderately prosperous society in all respects, proposed new requirements that were more policy-oriented, relevant to development problems and responsive to people's needs. These goals and requirements are consistent with the task of building a moderately prosperous society in all respects proposed by the 16th National Congress and new requirements outlined by the 17th National Congress. They also fit into the overall picture of socialism with Chinese characteristics.

6. Ensuring a decisive victory in building a moderately prosperous society in all respects

The period from the 19th National Congress in 2017 to December, 2020 witnessed efforts to ensure a decisive victory in building a moderately prosperous society in all respects and the start of a new journey toward fully building a modern socialist country. Efforts were focused on winning the three critical battles, especially the battle against poverty.

General Secretary Xi Jinping pointed out in the report to the 19th National Congress that by the time we celebrate our centenary, we will have developed our society into a moderately prosperous one with a stronger economy, greater democracy, more advanced science and education, thriving culture, greater social harmony, and a better quality of life. After this, with another 30 years of work, and by the time we celebrate the centenary of the People's Republic of China, we will have basically achieved modernization and turned China into a modern socialist country.

7. From finishing the building of a moderately prosperous society in all respects to fully building a modern socialist country

As pointed out in the Fifth Plenary Session of the 19th Central Committee of the CPC, the 14th Five-Year Plan period is the first five years in which we will embark on a new journey of fully building a modern socialist country and realizing the second centenary goal, after finishing building a moderately prosperous society in all respects and achieving the first centenary goal. China has entered a new development phase. The Fifth Plenary Session of the 19th CPC Central Committee drew a new blueprint for China's development in the new stage and put forward the grand vision of fully building a modern socialist country. This is a program of action for China to make continuous efforts towards the second centenary goal.

The above historical evolution tells that a moderately prosperous society has always been the goal throughout the over 40 years of reform and opening-up, from "Xiaokang Society" proposed by Deng Xiaoping to implementing the three-step strategy for achieving socialist modernization in China, from ensuring that people's basic needs are met to well-off society, from initial prosperity to moderate prosperity in all respects, to the decisive stage of finishing the building of a moderately prosperous society in all respects after the 18th National Congress of the CPC and achieving the goal of finishing the building of a moderately prosperous society in all respects in 2020. This path reflects the continuity of the CPC to achieve its goals and different features of the task in different stages, driving the transformation from initial prosperity to general prosperity, from low level to high level, and from quantitative to qualitative improvement.

II. New developments in the important statements on finishing the building of a moderately prosperous society in all respects

Since the 18th CPC National Congress, General Secretary Xi Jinping has made many important statements on finishing the building of a moderately prosperous society in all respects on different occasions. *Excerpts of Xi Jinping's Statements on Finishing the Building of a Moderately Prosperous Society in All Respects* alone includes 332 paragraphs from speeches, conversations, remarks, letters of congratulation, and instructions made by General Secretary Xi from November 15, 2012 to March 10, 2016. He introduced the goal to the international community at international events. He explained the vision to the general public in simple terms. He elaborated on priorities and challenges from a practical perspective. He enriched and expanded its dimensions in an effort to meet people's needs. There are also statements expounding on the significance of realizing general prosperity in China's overall economic and social development. These statements imply new thinking, add new dimensions to finishing the building of a moderately prosperous society in all respects, and demonstrate that the CPC constantly inherits, enriches and gives new meaning to its goal, showcasing the ability to progress with the times.

1. Drawing a new signpost: a critical step to realize the Chinese Dream

To achieve the rejuvenation of the Chinese nation has always been the greatest dream of our nation since modern times. According to documentation, achieving the rejuvenation of the Chinese nation was first mentioned in the report to the 13th National Congress of the CPC. In his remarks at the First Session of the 12th National People's Congress convened on March 17, 2013, General Secretary Xi Jinping said that to achieve the goals of finishing the building of a moderately prosperous society in all respects and building a modern socialist country that is prosperous, strong, democratic, culturally advanced, harmonious, and beautiful, and to realize the Chinese Dream of national rejuvenation means that we should strive for national renewal and prosperity, and deliver a happy life for our people. It represents the current aspirations of the Chinese people and the glorious tradition of our forefathers to constantly pursue progress. The above statement links the task of finishing the building of a moderately prosperous society in all respects closely with the goal of realizing the Chinese Dream.

"We have set the goal that we will finish the building of a moderately prosperous society in all respects by the 100th anniversary of the founding of the CPC, finish the building of a modern socialist country that is prosperous, strong, democratic, culturally advanced, harmonious, and beautiful, and strive to realize the Chinese Dream of national rejuvenation by the 100th anniversary of the founding of the PRC," General Secretary Xi Jinping elaborated on the task of finishing the building of a moderately prosperous society in all respects from the perspective of realizing the Chinese Dream at a meeting with national model workers on April 28, 2013.

These statements further enriched and took forward the goal of the Chinese Dream by bringing it in sync with the times, pointing out the path forward and clarifying requirements of practice.

2. Summarizing new features: to cover the largest population and most extensive areas

General Secretary Xi Jinping has many statements on "in all respects".

"All respects" means that all the population and regions should be covered and no one be left behind. It also means that our efforts to promote coordinated economic, political, cultural, social, and ecological advancement should also cover all respects. During a visit to those living in difficulty in Fuping County of Hebei Province on December 29, 2012, Xi Jinping said that the most daunting challenge lying in the way of finishing the building of a moderately prosperous society in all respects is in rural areas, especially in impoverished areas. The building of a moderately prosperous society in all respects would not be finished if rural areas, impoverished areas in particular, were not included. (*Remarks During the Inspection Tour to Fuping of Hebei Province for Development-oriented Poverty Reduction*, Central Party Literature Press, 2015, page 16) At a meeting with representatives from Gongshan Derung-Nu Autonomous County of Nujiang Prefecture in Kunming on January 20, 2015, Xi Jinping emphasized: "No ethnic groups should be excluded from a moderately prosperous society in all respects." "We would not say that we have achieved the first centenary goal and finished the building of a moderately prosperous society in all respects if such prosperity is not enjoyed by old revolutionary base areas, especially when the impoverished population in these areas have not been lifted out of poverty. This is why I say that when defining a moderately prosperous society, the key is to observe the condition of farmers." (*Bearing the Development of Old Revolutionary Base Areas in Mind—Sidelights on the Meeting of Poverty Reduction in Shaanxi-Gansu-Ningxia Old Revolutionary Base Areas Chaired by General Secretary Xi Jinping*) In his remarks delivered at the 2015 Global Poverty Reduction and Development Forum on October 16, 2015, Xi Jinping pointed out that a moderately prosperous society in all respects should benefit all Chinese people and no one should be left behind.

A moderately prosperous society in all respects also covers the most extensive areas. "Going forward, China will march towards two grand goals: the first is to ensure GDP and per capita rural and urban income in 2020 double that in 2010 and finish the building of a moderately prosperous society in all respects that benefits over one billion people; the second is to finish the building of a modern socialist country that is prosperous, strong, democratic, culturally advanced, harmonious, and beautiful as we celebrate the 100th anniversary of the PRC in 2049. Following a people-centered philosophy, we will promote coordinated economic, political, cultural, social, and ecological advancement, and find greater synergy among all stakeholders and all links in our modernization drive, and build a beautiful China," Xi Jinping said at the fifth meeting with BRICS leaders on March 27, 2013. Finishing the building of a moderately prosperous society in all respects requires that we should ensure: officials are honest, government is clean, and political affairs are handled with integrity; find the largest common ground in the need of aspirations of our people; the material and cultural strengths of the nation are on the rise and the material and cultural wellbeing of people of all ethnic groups is improved; the general public enjoy justice and fairness in every judicial case; the people live in a sound natural environment; and a moderately prosperous society serves as a strong pillar for realizing the Chinese Dream. Finishing the building of a moderately prosperous society in all respects covers five areas of economic, political, cultural, social, and ecological advancement.

3. Unfolding the defining feature: development

General Secretary Xi Jinping made several statements on the issue of development and pointed out that development is the defining feature of building a moderately prosperous society in all respects. On January 1, 2014, he made important remarks that in an effort to finish the building of a moderately prosperous society in all respects, realize socialist modernization and the great rejuvenation of the Chinese nation, the most fundamental and pressing task is to further unleash and develop productive forces; freeing our minds and unleashing productivity and social vitality aim to better unleash and develop productive forces; we should deepen reform to enable a great increase in dynamism of such factors as labor, knowledge, technology, management, and capital, and tap into all sources of social wealth. (*Xi Jinping: Acting on the Guiding Principles of the Third Plenary Session of the 18th CPC Central Committee,* No. 1 2014, *Qiushi*) In his speech at the National Congress of Brazil on July 16, 2014, Xi Jinping said, "The Chinese people are working hard to fulfill the Chinese dream of the great rejuvenation of the Chinese nation; China is the world's largest developing country; development is the key to solving all our country's problems."

The report to the 19th National Congress of the CPC mentioned the defining feature of a moderately prosperous society: the evolution of the principal contradiction facing Chinese society does not change our assessment of the present stage of socialism in China; the basic dimension of the Chinese context—that our country is still and will long remain in the primary stage of socialism—has not changed; China's international status as the world's largest developing country has not changed. These 3 aspects tell the defining feature of China's national conditions and determine that the most fundamental task is to concentrate on developing productive forces and development is the key to solving all our country's problems.

China has been making progress in development with different priorities. From 1978 to 1997, the priority was to resolve stalling development, the issue of poverty and backwardness. From 1997 to 2012, the priority was to speed up development. Since the 18th National Congress of the CPC was convened, the priority has been to address problems related to rapid development. At present, China's economy has been transitioning from rapid growth to high-quality development. It requires us to raise total factor productivity and realize general prosperity while pursuing high quality and efficiency.

4. New dimensions: people's health

On August 31, 2013, General Secretary Xi Jinping met with delegates attending meetings in honor of outstanding organizations and persons of recreational sports, and outstanding groups and workers of sports system. He pointed out that fitness-for-all programs were the foundation for people to stay fit and healthy, and good health of our people was a major part of a moderately prosperous society and the basis for personal development and a happy life. During his visit to a public health clinic in Shiwei Town, Dantu District, Zhenjiang City, Jiangsu Province, on December 13, 2014, General Secretary Xi Jinping learned about the development of medical care and health in rural areas and medical treatment to villagers. He met with villagers under treatment and stressed that a moderately prosperous society cannot be built without good health of all. These remarks have bonded together the goal of the CPC, life and future of every family and individual.

In the wake of the onslaught of COVID-19 last year, General Secretary Xi Jinping cared deeply about people's life and health, and made a number of instructions and remarks. He stressed that we always put people's lives and health front and center in our response to the outbreak, and acted decisively to contain the spread of the virus with effective measures. He pointed out that protecting the life and health of the people is a major mission of the Party's governance. (*Remarks Made by Xi Jinping at the 12th Meeting of the Central Commission for Comprehensively Deepening Reform*) The remarks have not only added new dimensions to a moderately prosperous society, but also elevated people's health to the level of governance.

5. The role of finishing the building of a moderately prosperous society in all respects in the four-pronged comprehensive strategy

The four-pronged comprehensive strategy is characterized by systemic and strategic perspectives. Finishing the building of a moderately prosperous society in all respects, deepening reform in all areas, advancing law-based governance, and strengthening strict self-governance of the Party are not in parallel. The latter three are actions while the first is a strategic goal leading the whole effort. Only by deepening reform in all areas and breaking the impediments of vested interests, can we generate drivers to build a moderately prosperous society; only by advancing law-based governance, establishing rules and order, promoting fairness and justice, can we underpin a moderately prosperous society; only by strengthening strict self-governance of the Party, forging the leadership core, and providing political support, can we ensure a moderately prosperous society.

The Fifth Plenary Session of the 19th CPC Central Committee developed "finishing the building of a moderately prosperous society in all respects" in the four-pronged comprehensive strategy into "building a modern socialist country", bonding together 2 centenary goals.

III. Embarking on a new journey to fully build a modern socialist country

Finishing the building of a moderately prosperous society in all respects is an important goal of China's socialist modernization. According to the report to the 19th National Congress of the CPC, the timeframes of the two centenary goals converge between the 19th and the 20th National Congress. In this period, not only must we finish building a moderately prosperous society in all respects and achieve the first centenary goal; we must also build on this achievement to embark on a new journey toward the second centenary goal of fully building a modern socialist country. This shows that finishing building a moderately prosperous society is a starting point for embarking on a new journey.

The report also points out that "From 2020 to 2035, we will build on the foundation created by the moderately prosperous society with a further 15 years of hard work to see that socialist modernization is basically realized. From 2035 to the middle of the 21st century, we will, building on having basically achieved modernization, work hard for a further 15 years and develop China into a great modern socialist country that is prosperous, strong, democratic, culturally advanced, harmonious, and beautiful." This shows that finishing building a moderately prosperous society, as a new starting point, carries a far-reaching impact and serves as a milestone of China's socialist modernization.

Finishing building a moderately prosperous society and eliminating absolute poverty, the great achievements that go down in history, have ushered in a grand and magnificent journey. This is a great and glorious accomplishment for the Chinese people, for the Communist Party of China, and for the Chinese nation! Over the past 100 years of struggle, Chinese Communists have stay committed to its founding mission and forged ahead with perseverance. Finishing building a moderately prosperous society is not the end. It is a starting point of a new life and a new endeavor.

The year 2021 marks the new journey toward fully building a modern socialist country and a new development stage of China. In this new development stage, we march toward the second centenary goal of fully building a modern socialist country. In his remarks at a study session at the Party School of the CPC Central Committee attended by provincial and ministerial-level officials on January 11, 2021, General Secretary Xi Jinping pointed out, "The new development stage remains in the primary stage of socialism, but it is also a new starting point built on decades of development. In this stage, the CPC has led the people in achieving the historic transformation from standing up and growing prosperous to becoming strong. It is a major stage in the development of socialism in China. The primary stage of socialism is not static, but rather dynamic, active, promising and permeated with vigorous vitality. It is a process of tiered progress and development."

2021 is the first year of the 14th Five-Year Plan. It is of great importance to get off to a good start. General General Xi Jinping stresses that it is our strategic vision for developing socialism with Chinese characteristics in the new era: firstly finish building a moderately prosperous society in all respects, then move on to basically realizing modernization, and then turn to making China a great modern socialist country in every dimension. We must work with resolve and tenacity, strive to begin a new journey toward fully building a modern socialist country, and write a brilliant chapter on our new journey to socialist modernization.

目　录

Contents

希望的田野

A Land of Promise

奔向小康的拖拉机

1979 年，沂蒙老区一辆老式拖拉机上载满了收获的粮食，上面围坐着喜获丰收的村民们。

1978 年 12 月，党的十一届三中全会召开之后，改革开放的东风迅速吹遍了神州大地，尤其是 1979 年邓小平提出"小康之家"后，人们对美好生活的憧憬在城市和乡村传递，人们满怀热情奔向幸福、奔向小康。

农忙时耕地，农闲时运输，拖拉机成为老百姓的"财源"。开上拖拉机的农民们满面春风，握紧方向盘，也把即将到来的殷实生活紧紧把控在自己手中。改革之风猎猎吹起，一台台拖拉机载满了袋袋食粮，载满了建造新房的水泥砖瓦，更是载满了人们奔向小康生活的蓬勃希望。

李百军 摄

A tractor laden with hope

Happy villagers are on an old tractor loaded with harvested grains in the old revolutionary base area of Yimeng in 1979.

In December 1978, after the Third Plenary Session of the 11th CPC Central Committee was held, reform and opening-up quickly rolled out across the country. In particular, after Deng Xiaoping presented the vision of building a society of general prosperity in 1979, in pursuit of a better life, people in both urban and rural areas have been marching towards happiness and a better-off life with great enthusiasm.

Tractors became a source of income for the people, used on farmland in busy seasons and for transportation in slack seasons. As they held the wheel of the tractors, the farmers were put on the driving seat of their own life. As reform went on, tractors were not only laden with grains and cement bricks, but also people's hope for a more prosperous life.

Photo by Li Baijun

敢为人先的小井村

1978 年，东明县小井村、柳里村在全省率先实行"大包干"。这是 1980 年小井村丰收的场景。

"大包干"是农村家庭联产承包责任制的雏形，东明县开风气之先，极大地调动了农民的生产积极性，在短时间内就取得了丰硕成果。截至 1980 年 9 月，各种类型的生产责任制已在东明县普遍开花，生产力得到了大幅度提升。当年全县粮食总产突破 2.5 亿斤，比 1979 年增长 5.9%；棉花总产 450 万斤，花生总产 1500 万斤，芝麻总产 300 万斤，分别比 1979 年增长 221%、320%、232%。

农户尝到了改革的甜头。家家粮满囤、谷满仓，农民们洋溢着丰收的喜悦。人们喜气洋洋地说："过去恐着没饭吃，现在愁着粮食没处放。""联产联住心，一年大翻身。红薯换蒸馍，光棍娶老婆。"

1980 年 11 月，《人民日报》刊载文章《阳光道与独木桥——试谈包产到户的由来、利弊、性质和前景》，列举了安徽省肥西县、山东省东明县实行包产到户的做法，作为全国学习的典范。

Xiaojing Village, a trailblazer

In 1978, Xiaojing Village and Liuli Village of Dongming County took the lead in implementing the contract system for agricultural production in the whole province. This is the scene of harvest in Xiaojing Village in 1980.

The all-round contract system for agricultural production was the initial form of the household contract responsibility system in rural areas. Dongming County was the first to implement the system, which greatly motivated the farmers' enthusiasm for production and achieved fruitful results in a short period of time. As of September 1980, various types of production responsibility systems had been established across Dongming County, and productivity had been significantly improved. In 1980, the county's total grain output exceeded 125,000 tons, an increase of 5.9% over that of 1979; the total output of cotton, peanuts, and sesame reached 2,250 tons, 7,500 tons, and 1,500 tons respectively, an increase of 221%, 320%, and 232% over that of 1979.

Reform delivered real benefits to the farmers. Barns were filled with grains, and farmers were full of joy for the bumper harvest. People joked that "We used to fear not having enough food to eat, but now we worry about not having enough room to store the food", and "The household contract responsibility system transformed our lives in just one year. Now we can eat steamed buns instead of sweet potatoes, and even a bachelor who had difficulties finding a wife now gets married."

In November 1980, the *People's Daily* published an article with a title of *The Broad Avenue and the Difficult Path—An Exploration into the Origin, Advantages and Disadvantages, Nature and Prospects of the Contract System for Agricultural Production*, which set the practices of Feixi County of Anhui Province and Dongming County of Shandong Province as national models.

不收粮票的"油条"

1980 年，卖油条的食品摊。引人注意的是，摊主在醒目的地方注明"不收粮票，每斤 6 角"。

在计划经济体制下，粮票是购买食品的凭证，没有粮票，寸步难行。

党的十一届三中全会后，随着改革的逐步深入，市场上各类物资慢慢丰富起来。经营小本生意的商贩们也自发在路边摆开了摊子，与此同时，人们开始重新认识商品经济。随之而来的是，严格的票证制度越来越松动，国家逐步缩小消费品定量配给的范围。

事实证明，20 世纪 80 年代的商品经济正是中国市场经济的开端。"建立自觉运用价值规律的计划体制，发展社会主义商品经济"，这是社会主义经济理论上的重大突破。

郑曙光 摄

No more food rationing

At a food stall selling deep-fried dough sticks in 1980, the stall owner puts up a sign saying "No food stamps. 6 *jiao* for every 0.5 kilograms."

Under the planned economy system, it was almost impossible to buy food without food stamps.

After the Third Plenary Session of the 11th CPC Central Committee, with the deepening of reform, more and more products were available on the market. Vendors who ran small businesses set up stalls at the roadside. People began to reacquaint themselves with the commodity economy. The strict stamp system gradually loosened up, and the country gradually reduced the scope of rationing of consumer goods.

Facts proved that the commodity economy in the 1980s was the beginning of China's market economy. The idea to establish a planned system that consciously uses the laws of value and develops a socialist commodity economy was a major breakthrough in socialist economic theory.

Photo by Zheng Shuguang

第一次拿到这么多钱

1980 年，聊城县许营公社农民喜领售棉款。第一次拿到这么多钱，母亲蹲在地上高兴地数了起来。

改革开放初期，聊城县委解放思想，在工作指导上由"以粮为纲"转为"粮棉一起抓，重点抓棉花"，大力发展多种经营，并在全县推广"大包干"制度。许营公社在全县较早实行包产到户，农民们的干劲儿像开闸的春水一般汹涌奔流，大家一门心思扑在发家致富上。1980 年，许营公社棉花大丰收。当年年底，许营公社举行售棉款集中发放大会，手捧厚厚的现金，棉农们喜在心里、笑在脸上。依靠种棉，不少棉农成为改革开放初期的"万元户"。

赵雅军 摄

So much cash for the first time

In 1980, a mother, holding so much money in hand for the first time, is counting the cash happily at the event that farmers from Xuying Commune in Liaocheng County receive the money for cotton sales.

In the early stage of reform and opening-up, the CPC Committee of Liaocheng County freed their minds, shifted the work priority from grains only to grains and cotton with the focus on cotton, vigorously diversified their economy, and promoted the all-round contract system for agricultural production across the county. The commune was one of the first to implement the household-based contract system for agricultural production in the county. Farmers were, therefore, more dedicated to pursing a better life. In 1980, the commune reaped a bumper cotton harvest. In the end of that year, it held an event to distribute the cash from cotton sales, for which the farmers were jubilant and looked truly radiant. By growing cotton, many farmers earned more than 10,000 yuan in the early stages of reform and opening-up.

Photo by Zhao Yajun

供销社送货到俺家门口

物资匮乏的年代，供销社里的东西很多时候都很紧俏，逢年过节前来购物的人更是摩肩接踵。很多商品都要在到货前几天在供销社门口竖起个牌子提前通知，到货当天一大早就会有很多人来排队购买，而且往往来晚了就买不到了。

供销社里销售日常用品如布匹、搪瓷脸盆和口杯等，文化用品如作业簿、铅笔、橡皮擦等，食品如面条、红糖、白糖等，在那个年代供不应求。

随着计划经济向市场经济转变，商品供应的日益充足，供销社也从辉煌的位子上退了下来,在激烈的市场竞争中,它也开始改变,寻找新的生存之路。

曾乃义 摄

Buy what I need at doorstep

In the era of supply shortage, products sold by the supply and marketing cooperatives were often in high demand, and shopping during holidays were even more crowded. The supply and marketing cooperative had to put up a notice a few days before the arrival of the goods. Many people would line up early in the morning on the day the goods arrived, and often found products sold out if they were late.

Supply often fell short of demand in those years for daily necessities such as cloth, enamel washbasins and cups, stationery such as exercise books, pencils, erasers, and food such as noodles, brown sugar, and white sugar.

As the planned economy transitioned to the market economy, the supply of goods became increasingly abundant. The supply and marketing cooperatives, confronted with the fierce market competition and losing their dominant position, and began to embrace changes and find new ways of survival.

Photo by Zeng Naiyi

俺们也"下海"了

1981年，沂蒙老区的妇女们推着载重自行车，带着她们精心准备的货物，踏入市场。

随着温饱问题逐渐解决，人们对生活质量充满更高的期许。与此同时，人们凝固的思维逐渐活跃起来。一些不甘于现状的农民大胆地走出本乡本土去闯世界。通过经商，一些祖祖辈辈面朝黄土背朝天的农民，很快富裕起来，过上了梦想中的富足生活。

在这样的潮流之下，以往安心在家相夫教子的妇女们心思也活络起来，她们勇敢地走出家门加入经商的大潮中。

李霞 摄

Women carry their goods to market

In 1981, women in the old revolutionary base area of Yimeng, push their bicycles loaded with goods in the market.

As the basic needs were gradually met, people began to have higher expectations for the quality of life. At the same time, people's mind also became more flexible. Some farmers, who were not satisfied with the status quo, boldly left their hometowns to the outside world to seek fortune. Through doing business, some farmers, whose ancestors relied on the farmland to make a living for generations, quickly became rich and led the well-to-do life they had dreamed of.

Against this backdrop, many women who used to be devoted housewives also became active, and bravely stepped out of the house to join the tide of business.

Photo by Li Xia

搬新家了

这是济南的一家三口,喜气洋洋地搬进了新房,房间里有了电视机、缝纫机、大衣柜,住房宽敞了,生活水平也提高了。

一条长长窄窄的走廊串连着许多个小小的房间,走廊两端通风,状如筒子,这就是几代城市居民的记忆居所——"筒子楼"。随着我国工业化、城镇化步伐的加快,城镇人口快速增加,20世纪80年代,城市居民的住宅开始多元化。

"我有一所房子,面朝大海,春暖花开……"海子的诗,描述了大多数人对生活的美好想象和现实追求。幸福是奋斗出来的,房子从"栖身之所"到"宜居之选"的蜕变,彰显了人民与日俱增的幸福感。

Move into a new home

A family of three in Jinan move into a new house happily. The room is equipped with a TV, a sewing machine, and a large closet. The more spacious room brings with it a better quality of life.

A long and narrow corridor connected many small rooms together, and the two ends of the corridor were ventilated and shaped like tubes. This is the tube-shaped building, which had lived in urban resident's memory for several generations. As industrialization and urbanization accelerated in China, the urban population increased rapidly. In the 1980s, the types of urban housing began to diversify.

"Living in a house facing the sea, with spring blossoms..." Haizi's poem describes most people's expectation for and pursuit in life. Happiness is the result of hard work. The transition of the houses from a shelter to a livable place demonstrates people's growing sense of happiness.

（上页图说）

条条致富路

改革开放的大潮中，农民们也逐渐脱离了田地的束缚，在商品经济中寻找致富之路。1982 年，31 岁的淄博农民朱永连靠着编精美实用的条筐劳动致富。1985 年，这幅照片获得联合国教科文组织第十届摄影比赛亚洲文化中心奖，国内外不少报刊也陆续刊登了这幅作品。照片中的朱永连成了当地的名人。大连一家出口公司从报纸上看到照片后，千方百计与朱永连取得联系，与他签订购销合同，包销他的全部条筐，朱永连一家的日子也红火起来。

在这张照片拍摄之后的数十年间，摄影师曾毅多次造访朱永连。时隔多年，朱永连家的生活发生了翻天覆地的变化。他们家已经搬到城里的一个高档社区，房子窗明几净，各类家电一应俱全。当年 6 岁的翠翠已成为青岛一家旅行社的导游，英语说得非常好。2015 年，《条条致富路》这幅见证历史的照片被美国第 39 任总统吉米·卡特收藏。

曾毅 摄

Weave a better life

In the tide of reform and opening-up, farmers gradually broke away from the shackles of the farmland and looked for ways towards a better life in the commodity economy. In 1982, 31-year-old Zhu Yonglian, a farmer in Zibo, became rich by weaving beautiful and handy baskets. This photo won the Asian Cultural Center Award of the 10th UNESCO Photo Contest in 1985, and was published on many newspapers and magazines at home and abroad, making Zhu Yonglian a local celebrity. After seeing the photo in the newspaper, an export company in Dalian found ways to get in touch with him and signed a sale contract with him to sell all his baskets, making the life of Zhu Yonglian's family more thriving.

In the decades after this photo was taken, the photographer Zeng Yi visited Zhu Yonglian many times. Over the years, the life of Zhu Yonglian's family has undergone huge changes. His family has moved to an upscale urban residential community with bright and clean rooms and various home appliances. Cuicui, who was 6 years old at the time the photo was taken, has become a tour guide for a travel agency in Qingdao and speaks fluent English. In 2015, this photo, a witness of the history, was collected by Jimmy Carter, the 39th President of the United States.

Photo by Zeng Yi

山东第一个"万元户"

临清县八岔路公社赵塔头村一队的"万元户"赵汝兰在购买北极星座钟。

在当时,"万元户"赵汝兰是当地的知名人物。赵汝兰承包了土地21亩,自己又开荒9亩,他把这30亩土地都种上了棉花。赵汝兰用的是"鲁棉一号"良种,每亩收获110千克,共收获3300千克,每斤售价2.6元,除去成本后收入达10239元。

1980年11月17日,新华社发表了一幅照片报道赵汝兰一家当年棉花纯收入过万元的消息,赵汝兰也成了山东首个见诸报端的"万元户"。这则报道先后被国内外多家新闻媒体采用,"万元户"一词也随之流行起来。卖棉成了"万元户",赵家不但衣食无忧,还添置了好多当时的"大件"——五辆自行车、三台缝纫机、两块手表、一台座钟、两台收音机,一共花了近2000元钱。

"万元户"是20世纪80年代初的流行词,也是很多农民羡慕的称谓,是先富起来的代名词。

李霞 摄

The first household with 10,000-yuan income in Shandong

Zhao Rulan, a woman with over 10,000-yuan asset from the first team of Zhaotatou Village, Bachalu Commune, Linqing County, buys a North Star clock.

At that time, Zhao Rulan was a well-known local figure. After contracting 14,000 square meters of land and opening up another 6,000 square meters of wasteland, she planted all the land with cotton using the "Lumian No. 1" cotton seed. It was calculated that by harvesting 3,300kg of cotton (110kg of cotton per 666 square meters), multiplied by 2.6 yuan per 0.5kg, Zhao's income reached 10,239 yuan after deducting the cost.

Xinhua News Agency published a photo reporting the news that Zhao Rulan's family had a net income of more than 10,000 yuan through cotton sales that year on November 17, 1980. Her family became the first 10,000-yuan household from Shandong reported in the newspapers. This report was adopted by many news media at home and abroad, and the term "10,000-yuan household" also became popular. By selling cotton, in addition to meeting the basic needs, the family also bought several big-ticket items, such as five bicycles, three sewing machines, two watches, a desk clock, and two radios, with nearly 2,000 yuan.

10,000-yuan household was a buzz word in the early 1980s. It was also the envy of many farmers, and a symbol of those who prospered first.

Photo by Li Xia

俺也买了时髦衣裳

1982 年，聊城冠县大区村妇女，穿着新衣服喜笑颜开。

人们的审美总是紧跟时代的步伐，与政治、经济、思想观念等紧密相连，改革开放后，经济上的迅猛发展和思想观念的更新嬗变直接影响到人们对美的理解与追求。

照片中，这户人家的女儿，围着长长的围巾，绕过一周，垂挂在胸前，这是 80 年代最时兴的围法。她穿的标准服，都是从商店买来布回家自己做的，鞋子是皮鞋，与她的母亲与奶奶比，她便是很现代了。而她的母亲，宽宽的肥肥的棉裤，传统的对襟袄，白羊肚的毛巾扎在头上。和老太太不同的是，她的棉衣棉裤，都有外罩，还有她的球鞋与老太太的小脚自然形成对比，老太太戴的棉帽在当时是整个华北地区流行的。三代人的服饰变化折射出经济的发展和时代的进步。

李锦 摄

My new dress

A woman in Daqu Village, Guanxian County, Liaocheng, smiles in new clothes in 1982.

People's taste in clothes changes with the progress of the times, and is closely connected with politics, economy, and values. Since reform and opening-up started, the rapid economic development and the evolution of ideas have directly affected people's understanding and pursuit of beauty.

In the photo, the daughter of this family wears a long scarf around her head and neck. This was the most fashionable way to wear a scarf in the 1980s. The standard clothes she wore were all cloths bought from the store and self-made. The shoes were leather-made. Compared with her mother and grandma, she is very stylish. Her mother wears loose cotton-padded trousers and a traditional cotton-padded jacket with a white towel tied to her head. Unlike the grandma, the mother's cotton-padded clothes and trousers have outer covers, and her sneakers form a stark contrast with the grandma's bound feet. The cotton cap worn by the grandma was popular throughout North China at that time. The clothing changes of the three generations reflect economic development and the progress of the times.

Photo by Li Jin

错不了

1984 年，昌邑县城年集上，小贩在用计算器给老大娘算账。

农村的集市是 80 年代农村经济大发展的一个侧影。农民的钱包鼓了，商品供应丰富了，大家伙儿都来赶集，买了很多平时舍不得买的东西。

随着生活水平的提高，超市出现了，日常用品一应俱全，人们可以一站式购齐。现在的农村也有了很多大型超市连锁店，集购物、休闲、娱乐于一体。

从集市到超市，从商品售卖、展示到便捷式购物、一站式购齐，人们生活水平的提高和商品经济的发展一目了然。

李锦 摄

This is the amount you should pay

A vendor uses a calculator to show the price to an old lady at the New Year's fair of Changyi County in 1984.

The rural market was an epitome of the great development of the rural economy in the 1980s. Farmers became richer and the supply of goods was increasingly abundant. They came to the fair and bought a lot of things that they usually thought were too expensive to buy.

With the improvement of living standards, supermarkets appeared with daily necessities readily available, and people could buy them all in one go. There were also many large supermarket chains in rural areas, integrating shopping, leisure and entertainment.

From fair to supermarket, and from merchandise sales and display to convenient shopping and one-stop shopping, the improvement of people's living standards and the development of the commodity economy are notable.

Photo by Li Jin

添了新大件

1986 年，抱着新购置的收录机的农村妇女们，喜不自禁。

20 世纪 80 年代，经济的快速发展鼓起了农村人的钱包。在温饱解决后，人们开始追求精神的愉悦，休闲成为一个真正展开的话题，成为时代响亮的、多彩的主题。电视机、收录机等家电开始进入农民的家庭。来自港台的电视剧、时尚音乐开始响彻在城乡大街小巷，人们的视野和审美都在悄然变化着。

庞守义 摄

Big-ticket items bought

The rural women holding the newly purchased radio and tape recorders are beaming with joy in 1986.

Farmers grew richer in the 1980s along with the rapid economic development. As the basic needs were met, people began to enrich their intellectual and cultural life. Leisure, a topic more and more people loved to talk about, became a resounding and colorful theme of the times. Home appliances, such as TV sets and radio cassette players, found their way to rural households. TV dramas and music from Hong Kong and Taiwan can be heard everywhere, and people's horizon and taste also changed gradually.

Photo by Pang Shouyi

俺们的学校大变样

　　沂南县界湖镇山庄小学的孩子们在课间做游戏。沂蒙山区改善教学条件，学生们告别土台子、石凳子。

　　20世纪80年代之前，山东很多农村的中小学校舍是黑屋子、危房子，用土台子、水泥板、砖头堆当课桌凳上课的学生达半数以上。自20世纪70年代末以来，山东各地逐步对农村中小学校舍进行改造。坚持"一无两有六配套"的标准，即中小学校舍要实现校校无危房，班班有教室，人人有课桌凳，校园内配套围墙、大门、操场、旗杆、水井、厕所。1000多万中小学生从此告别了黑屋子、土台子、危房子，走进了宽敞明亮的教室。许多地方还集资为学校建设了图书资料室、实验室，配备了文体器材，开辟了生产劳动基地，兴建了教师宿舍。

Big changes at school

Children play games between classes at Shanzhuang Primary School in Jiehu Town, Yinan County, after the teaching conditions were improved, and earthen platforms and stone stools become a thing of the past in the Yimeng mountainous area.

Before the 1980s, many rural primary and secondary school buildings in Shandong were dilapidated houses without access to electricity. More than half of the students used earthen platforms, cement boards, or brick piles as makeshift desks and stools. After the end of the 1970s, Shandong began to gradually renovate rural primary and secondary school buildings. The standard was that there should be no dilapidated buildings in primary and secondary schools, each class should have their own classroom, everyone should have desks and stools, and enclosures, gates, playgrounds, flagpoles, wells, and toilets should be put on every campus. Since then, more than 10 million primary and middle school students ended the days of going to dangerous houses with dark classrooms and earthen platforms, and walked into spacious and bright classrooms. Many places also raised funds to build school libraries and laboratories, purchased cultural and sport equipment, opened production bases, and built teachers' dormitories.

慎终追远

　　1986 年，曲阜孔庙祭孔大典现场。

　　祭孔是民间对孔子表达尊敬仰慕和追思的纪念活动。在仪式过程中，设音乐、舞蹈表演，并呈献牲、酒等祭品。在典仪官的主持下，大典分为"迎神""初献""亚献""终献"等六部分，集礼、乐、歌、舞为一体，生动再现了古代祭孔典礼，用艺术的形式集中表现了儒家思想文化，体现了艺术形式与文化内容的高度统一，形象地阐释了孔子学说中的"礼"的含义，表达了"仁者爱人""以礼立人"的思想，具有较强的思想亲和力、精神凝聚力和艺术感染力。发掘、抢救、保护和开发利用"祭孔大典"，对于弘扬优秀传统文化，营造和乐氛围，构建和谐社会，凝聚民族精神具有不可替代的社会价值，它所阐释的民族文化和民族精神的精髓，将对中国乃至华人世界的文化传播产生积极的影响。

孔红晏　摄

A ceremony to pay tribute to Confucius

A ceremony paying tribute to Confucius is held at the Confucian Temple in Qufu in 1986.

Worshiping Confucius is a commemorative activity to express people's respect and admiration for Confucius. During the ceremony, there are music and dance performances with animal and alcohol sacrifices. Hosted by the ceremonial official, the ceremony is divided into six parts, such as welcoming the gods, first offerings, second offerings and final offerings. By combining ritual, music, singing, and dance, it reproduces the ancient ceremony of worshiping Confucius, demonstrates the Confucian culture by integrating art and culture, vividly explains the meaning of ritual in Confucianism, and expresses the idea that "the benevolent loves others" and "one should learn good manners so as to behave properly", embodying the features of inclusiveness, cohesiveness and artistic appeal. The exploration, protection, and development of the ceremony has an irreplaceable social value for promoting fine traditional culture, creating a friendly atmosphere, building a harmonious society, and advancing the spirit of the nation. The essence of the national culture and spirit illustrated by the ceremony will have a positive impact on spreading the culture of China and the Chinese all over world.

Photo by Kong Hongyan

临沂商贸的蝶变

　　临沂尽管地处沂蒙山区，地理环境相对闭塞，但是改革的春风依然吹到了这里。不甘落后、勤劳朴实的沂蒙人民开始自发地在城乡人流比较集中的地方摆起了地摊，形成了临沂第一代集贸式市场。露天式的经营模式杂乱无章，不能遮风挡雨，因此 1987 年，在原临沂长途汽车站北，一座占地 6 万平方米，上空覆盖着塑料大棚，下方是一个个水泥台子的大型市场——临沂服装鞋帽批发市场横空出世，"西郊大棚底"的美名从此叫响。自此，以临沂服装鞋帽批发市场为中心，集家电、五金、塑料制品、文体用品等的专业批发市场如雨后春笋般纷纷建立，形成了规模宏大的市场集群，凝聚了国内同类市场难以匹敌的人气，临沂大商城初具雏形。经过三十多年的发展，传统的"西郊大棚"如今已经发展为现代化国际化的商城，临沂商城经过不断升级换代，成功实现了以商贸物流业为龙头带动区域经济社会全面发展的美丽蝶变。

李百军　摄

Thriving business in Linyi

Linyi, despite its relatively closed geographical location in the Yimeng mountainous area, still benefited from the reform. Unwilling to be left behind, the industrious and down-to-earth people of Yimeng began to set up stalls in places where the flow of urban and rural residents was relatively concentrated, forming the first-generation of market in Linyi. The open-air business model was chaotic and could not shelter people from the wind and rain. Therefore, the Linyi Garment, Shoe and Hat Wholesale Market with plastic sheds on the roof and concrete tables underneath was established in the north of the original Linyi Coach Station in 1987, covering an area of 60,000 square meters. Since then, surrounding this market, other special wholesale markets for home appliances, hardware, plastic products, and cultural and sports goods mushroomed and thrived in the city. With a large-scale market cluster and huge domestic popularity in China, the Linyi business complex took shape. After more than 30 years of development, the market has now developed into a modern and international shopping complex. After continuous upgrading, the complex has gone through a remarkable transformation, serving the regional economy and society with commerce and logistics as main drivers.

Photo by Li Baijun

俺们有了身份证

1987 年 12 月，利津县文化馆工作人员在为西王村民拍摄第一代身份证证件照。

新中国成立初期，中国公民没有居民身份证，证明自己身份的时候用的是户口簿和单位介绍信。1984 年 4 月 6 日，国务院批转公安部关于颁发居民身份证若干问题请示的通知，同时公布了《中华人民共和国居民身份证试行条例》。自此，中国通过实施居民身份证制度，开始对居民实施户口证件化管理。2004 年 1 月 1 日，应用 IC 卡技术、可机读的第二代居民身份证正式换发。身份证从无到有，从第一代发展到第二代，不仅是简单的个人身份证明的变化，方寸之间折射的是社会管理方式的转变和居民生活质量的提高，对于方便群众生活和保护公民合法权益都有重要意义。

黄利平 摄

Take photo to get my identity card

The staff of the Lijin County Cultural Center takes photos for the villagers of Xiwang to get the first generation ID card in December 1987.

In the early days of the People's Republic of China, Chinese citizens did not have their own ID card. They could only prove their identity with the household registration booklet and the letter of introduction from their employer. On April 6, 1984, the State Council approved and forwarded the notice of the Ministry of Public Security on the issuance of ID cards, and promulgated *Regulations on the Trial Implementation of ID Cards in the People's Republic of China*. Since then, China has begun to implement household registration file management through the ID card system. On January 1, 2004, the machine-readable second-generation ID card applying IC card technology was officially issued to replace the previous one. The development of ID card not only reflects the change in personal identification, but also shows the transformation in social management and improvement in the quality of life. It is of great significance for making people's life more convenient and protecting the legitimate rights and interests of citizens.

Photo by Huang Liping

俺们的大棚菜上市了

　　1989 年，寿光蔬菜批发市场开市。"寿光大棚菜上市了，上市了！"隆冬的寿光蔬菜市场上，两个摊贩站在汽车上，用竹竿挑着豆角、苹果、蒜薹高声叫卖。

　　寿光就是在这种原始的批发市场基础上一步步做大做强，最终成为全国的"菜篮子"。这个亚洲最大的农产品批发市场，每天都有 300 多个品种、15000 吨的新鲜果蔬，被运往全国 200 多个大中城市，或是直接装进集装箱，当天就上了国外的餐桌。今天，中国北方冬天的餐桌，早已走出了被萝卜白菜支配的恐惧，这是一个时代的进步，更是用蔬菜产业致富，同时改变亿万国人生活方式的故事。

李锦 摄

Sell vegetables grown in greenhouse

"Shouguang vegetables grown in greenhouses are available now," say two vendors standing on their vehicle and selling beans, apples, and garlic sprouts at the Shouguang Vegetable Market in midwinter when the Shouguang Vegetable Wholesale Market opens in 1989.

It is based on this primitive form of wholesale market that Shouguang grows in strength step by step and becomes a hub of vegetable production in China. As Asia's largest wholesale market for agricultural products, it supplies 15,000 tons of over 300 varieties of fresh fruits and vegetables every day to more than 200 large and medium-sized cities across the country, and to the dining tables in overseas households. Today, long gone are the days when the only vegetable people in the northern China could have in winter were radish and cabbage. It shows the progress of the times. More importantly, it tells a story of becoming prosperous through the vegetable industry and changing the life of hundreds of millions of people in the process.

Photo by Li Jin

多姿多彩的舜井街

1988 年 5 月 11 日，走在济南市舜井街步行大道上的服装模特表演队。

1978 年的改革之风，吹向全国，暖了济南这座古城。济南的城市风貌随之发生了翻天覆地的变化，人们的生活水平逐渐提高，衣着服饰从单一走向多元，日益丰富多彩。改革开放之前，由于物资匮乏，人们着装崇尚简朴，款式基本上是中山装、军便装、人民装、两用衫等，色彩主要是蓝、绿、灰，即"老三色"。随着时代的变化，20 世纪 80 年代，中国人的服装从"保守朴素、样式单一"逐步走向"热情开放、色彩斑斓"，人们开始接受并追求新颖的服装款式。随着济南经济快速发展，人们的衣着变化演绎了都市时尚，彰显了泉城的生机与活力。

郑立强 摄

Fashion Show in the street

Models walk on the Shunjing Street, Jinan City on May 11, 1988.

The reform was launched across the country in 1978, and brought vibrancy to Jinan, an ancient city. The city took on a completely new look, people's living standards were gradually improved, and the fashion style also grew diverse and colorful. Before the reform and opening-up was initiated, people preferred simple dresses due to supply shortage. The styles were basically Chinese tunic suit, military jacket, Mao jacket, dual-purpose shirts and others. The colors were mainly blue, green, and gray. With the change of the times, in the 1980s, the dressing style gradually changed from conservative, simple, and dull to enthusiastic, open and colorful, and people began to accept and pursue novel styles of clothing. With the rapid economic development of Jinan, the changes of people's dresses demonstrated urban fashion and the vitality of the City of Springs.

Photo by Zheng Liqiang

雪山引路人

1990 年 9 月，党员领导干部的楷模孔繁森同志在拉萨与藏族青年老师交谈。

在西藏十年，孔繁森始终把人民放在第一位，诠释了一名共产党员对人民的挚爱，诠释了民族团结的真谛。一代又一代援藏干部不畏艰难险阻，离开熟悉的小家，为西藏的发展费心尽力，为西藏人民的幸福出谋划策，充分展现了共产党人的执着和奉献。

庞守义 摄

Reaching out a helping hand to people in Tibet

Comrade Kong Fansen, a role model of Party leaders and officials, talks with a young Tibetan teacher in Lhasa in September 1990.

During his ten-year tenure in Tibet, Kong Fansen always put the people first, illustrating the deep bond between a Communist Party member and the people, and demonstrating the essence of national unity. Generations of officials selected to support the development of Tibet, despite difficulties and challenges, left their families and worked hard for Tibet and the happiness of the Tibetan people, speaking volumes about the perseverance and dedication of the Communists.

Photo by Pang Shouyi

学习雷锋好榜样

　　1990 年 3 月 4 日，山东财经学院的学生在学雷锋活动中走上街头为群众义务理发。

　　雷锋这个响亮的名字，伴随着"雷锋精神"，深深镌刻在一代又一代中国人的心中，影响和激励着一代又一代人成长。大学生响应党的号召，走进人民群众，为人民群众服务。他们走进乡村，开展形式多样的宣传活动，推动基层宣传思想工作不断开创新局面。他们走上街头，组成志愿服务大队，在改善公共秩序、维护公共环境卫生、共守文明交通等方面躬身实践，使市容市貌不断优化。如今，新时代的青年志愿者继续发扬"雷锋精神"，争当永不生锈的"螺丝钉"，为人民服务，让雷锋精神融入日常工作生活和岗位，在新时代的阳光下随风飘扬。

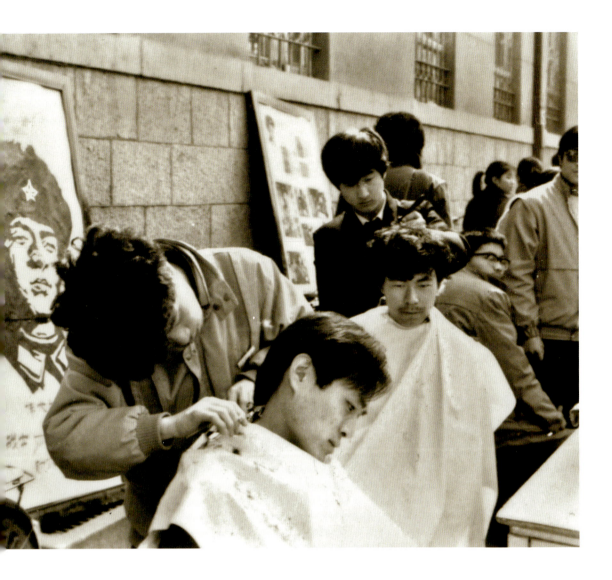

Follow the example of model soldier Lei Feng

Students from Shandong Economic University take to the streets to provide voluntary haircuts for people during the activity of learning from Lei Feng on March 4, 1990.

The resounding name of Lei Feng, along with the "Lei Feng Spirit", has been deeply engraved in the hearts of generations of Chinese people, influencing and inspiring several generations. Responding to the Party's call to get close to and serve the people, college students went to the countryside to carry out various forms of publicity activities and made new advances in community-level publicity. They also formed volunteer service teams to help improve public order and environmental sanitation, and maintain orderly traffic in cities. Today, young volunteers of the new era are committed to carrying forward the "Lei Feng Spirit" in work and daily life, shouldering their due responsibility and serving the people.

"海上山东" 乘风破浪

20 世纪 90 年代，山东船企为德国客商建造的万吨集装箱货轮举行下水仪式。

新中国成立后，特别是改革开放以来，山东积极开发建设海洋，20 世纪 90 年代率先启动"海上山东"建设跨世纪工程。它突破了传统海洋发展观念，放眼于世界与未来，与山东的经济强省发展目标相结合，促进了全省经济发展。

在"海上山东"开发建设规划中，政府明确提出了发展船舶工业的战略构想。进入 21 世纪以来，山东省政府进一步提出将"船舶链"作为全省重点发展的"四大产品链"之一，力争用 3 年至 5 年的时间，把船舶工业发展成为全省经济新的战略增长点，将山东省建成船舶工业大省。

召立智 摄

A huge container ship built for a German company

A Shandong vessel manufacturer holds a launching ceremony for the 10,000-ton container ship built for a German client in the 1990s.

After the founding of the People's Republic of China, especially since the reform and opening-up, Shandong has been active in developing the marine industry. In the 1990s, the province launched the project of Maritime Shandong. Moving beyond the traditional idea of ocean development, the project adopted an international and future-oriented vision, and synergized with the goal of making Shandong an economically strong province.

In the plan of Maritime Shandong, the government clearly put forward the strategic vision of developing the shipbuilding industry. Since the beginning of the 21st century, the Shandong Provincial Government has proposed to make the shipping chain one of the four major product chains of the province, and take 3 to 5 years to develop the shipbuilding industry into a new source of economic growth and make Shandong a major shipbuilding powerhouse.

Photo by Zhao Lizhi

俺们把荒山秃岭变成了"金山银山"

1992 年 4 月 16 日，莱芜腰关乡西巍石村率先在全省施行荒山拍卖，54 岁的陈老汉用 260 元租赁下了 50 亩荒山，沉睡了多年的荒山秃岭陆续被农民改变为"金山银山"。

作为集体财产的重要一部分，荒山归属集体所有，由集体统一经营管理。但由于受益主体和管理主体不明确，调动不起农民的积极性。20 世纪 90 年代，随着农村经济改革的深化，农村一些地方从强化农业基础地位与增强农业后劲着眼，开始推出拍卖荒山新举措，通过拍卖荒山的使用权、管理权，明确了产权关系，把荒山开发与农民自身利益紧密联系了起来，从而掀起农村土地"二次开发"热潮。实践证明，此举不仅对推动山区开发建设有着十分显著的作用，而且为农民脱贫致富开辟了途径。它对深化农村改革，优化资源配置，健全和完善农村土地市场体系，加速农村经济发展，产生了深远影响。

高留声 摄

Bidding to cultivate barren hills

The 54-year-old Chen spends 260 yuan to lease 33,333 square meters of barren mountains on April 16, 1992, at Xiweishi Village, Yaoguan Township, Laiwu, which is the first village to auction barren mountains in the province. The barren hills and mountains, untapped for so many years, are turned into invaluable assets by farmers.

As an important part of collective property, barren mountains were collective-owned and managed. Farmers' enthusiasm could not be mobilized because the beneficiaries and management entities were not clearly defined. In the 1990s, with the deepening of the economic reform in rural areas, some rural areas, with a focus on strengthening the fundamental role of agriculture and generating sustained momentum for agricultural development, began to take new measures like auctioning barren hills. By auctioning the rights to use and management, property rights were clearly defined, and barren hill development and farmers' interests were closely bonded, creating a strong wave of redevelopment of rural land. Facts proved that this approach not only played a significant role in promoting the development of mountainous areas, but also opened up new ways to lead farmers out of poverty. It had a profound impact on deepening rural reforms, optimizing resource allocation, strengthening and improving the rural land market system, and accelerating rural economic development.

Photo by Gao Liusheng

山东迈入"高速时代"

1993 年，济青高速济南零点立交桥建成。

济青高速正式通车，标志着山东公路建设进入了"高速时代"。

1998 年，山东交通发起了第一个"150 战役"，当年完成公路建设投资 153.5 亿元，全省高速公路通车总里程达 914 公里，跃居全国第一位。2002 年 9 月，莱新高速公路建成，高速公路通车里程达到 2411 公里，成为全国率先实现"省会与各市驻地通高速"的省份，构筑起以济南为中心的"半日生活圈"。2007 年 12 月，青兰高速公路青岛至莱芜段竣工通车，全省高速公路突破 4000 公里，一个以省会济南为枢纽，贯通各市，连接周边省份的"五纵四横一环"的高速公路网主骨架基本形成。截至 2020 年底，全省高速公路总里程达到 7473 公里。

在这片充满魅力的土地上，一条条公路宛如一条条缎带，为齐鲁大地增添了无限生机和活力，加快了山东融入世界的步伐。

汤序民 摄

A network of expressways takes shape in Shandong

In 1993, the construction of Lingdian Overpass on the Jinan-Qingdao Expressway is completed.

The inauguration of Jinan-Qingdao Expressway marks the start of a "high-speed era" of highway construction in Shandong.

In 1998, the first "Campaign of 15 Billion Yuan" was launched and, at the end of the year, a total of 15.35 billion yuan was invested in highway construction and the expressway mileage hit 914 kilometers, the longest in China. In September 2002, the Laiwu-Xintai Expressway was completed, and the expressway mileage in Shandong reached 2,411 kilometers. Shandong became the first province where the provincial capital city was connected to every city in the province by expressways, and since then a "half day life circle" with Jinan at the center took shape. In December 2007, the Qingdao-Laiwu section of the Qingdao-Lanzhou Expressway was completed and opened to traffic, making the expressway mileage of the whole province exceed 4,000 kilometers. An expressway network was formed ever since, with five expressways going from south to east, four from east to west, and one circling around the province. They run through cities in Shandong with Jinan as the hub and connect neighboring provinces. As of the end of 2020, the expressway mileage in Shandong reached 7,473 kilometers.

The roads are like ribbons, adding vitality to this charming land and accelerating the integration of Shandong into the world.

Photo by Tang Xumin

俺们也爱赶时髦

　　1993 年，临沂农村大集上，几个年轻的农村姑娘买了新衣服。漂亮的耳环、精巧的项链把姑娘们点缀得犹如春天里盛开的花朵。她们脸上稍显稚嫩、羞赧的表情遮盖不住洋溢的青春，对时尚、美丽的追求，是她们美好生活的缩影。

　　八九十年代，富裕起来的农民开始，对美有了新的追求，喇叭裤、蝙蝠衫、健美裤、连衣裙逐渐流行开来，农村姑娘的衣着越来越时尚。

李百军 摄

New dresses just bought

In 1993, at a rural fair in Linyi, several young rural girls buy new clothes. Beautiful earrings and delicate necklaces embellish them with shy and blooming cheeks. They look like spring flowers in full blossom. Their pursuit of fashion and beauty is a reflection of their dream of a better life.

In the 1980s and 1990s, better-off farmers became fashion conscious. Flared pants, bat-sleeved shirts, tight pants and dresses became more popular, and the clothing of rural girls became more and more fashionable.

Photo by Li Baijun

千里银线送深情

1996年，山东最后一批无电户实现合闸通电。费县方城镇西红峪自然村8家农户在自家门口张贴"千里银线送深情，万家灯火谢党恩"的对联。

在此之前，因电力发展不均，山东部分农村经济发展受到严重制约，1995年政府出资兴建"户户通电"工程，确保每一户农民都能用上电。1998年，山东开始实施农网改造工程，让农民用上安全电。近年来，随着农村居民生活水平的提高和农业现代化的快速发展，全省上下开展了一轮又一轮的农网升级改造，开启电力扶贫攻坚新篇章。

王剑 摄

Every village in Shandong now has access to electricity

In 1996, the last batch of households without access to power in Shandong is power-on. In celebration, eight farmers in Xihongyu Ziran Village, Fangcheng Town, Fei County, post couplet on their door, "Miles of cable transmit electricity to our village, thousands of lights gleam with gratitude to the Party."

The lack of electricity had slowed down the development of the economy in some rural areas of Shandong Province. In 1995, the government funded and started the campaign of "Electricity in Every Household" to ensure every family in the countryside was powered up. In 1998, Shandong began to rebuild the power grid in the countryside, providing everyone safe access to electricity. As the living standards in the countryside drastically improved and agriculture rapidly modernized, the power grid in Shandong has been upgraded multiple times, writing a new chapter of fuelling poverty alleviation through electricity.

Photo by Wang Jian

电气化改变农民生活

　　1998年1月，临沂市河东区相公镇刘团村成为全省第一个电气化村，全村实现了点灯不用油、做饭不用柴、取暖不用煤的电气化生活方式。

　　村镇电气化的发展，缩短了人们从事家务和生产劳作的时间，改变了农民的生产、生活方式。

王剑 摄

Electric appliances are common in kitchens of rural families

In January 1998, Liutuan Village, Xianggong Town, Hedong District, Linyi, becomes the first electrified village in the whole province.

For the first time, villagers lighted lamps without kerosene, cooked without firewood, and heated their house without burning coal. As more and more villages were electrified, people spent less time on housework and farming. The way of production and lifestyles of farmers have since then been changed.

Photo by Wang Jian

"双冠王"

1999 年 12 月 12 日，鲁能泰山队以 3 ∶ 2 的比分战胜大连万达队，赢得足协杯冠军，从而获得中国足球职业联赛史上第一个"双冠王"。

鲁能泰山队从此成为中国足坛不可或缺的一部分，引领山东人民以更加积极昂扬的姿态开展体育事业。随后的 20 余年里，山东全面深化体育事业改革，不断完善基本公共服务体系，体育强省建设步伐迈得铿锵有力，全民健身事业蓬勃发展，竞技体育事业蒸蒸日上，体育产业发展势头正盛。

庞守义 摄

Double championships won by Shandong football team

On December 12, 1999, Luneng Taishan defeats Dalian Wanda with a score of 3:2 and won the CFA Cup, becoming the first team winning two titles in a single season in the history of the Chinese professional football league.

Luneng Taishan has since become an indispensable part of Chinese football, inspiring more active engagement of Shandong people in sports. In the following 20 years, Shandong has made more sport industry reforms, and continuously improved the basic public service system. Solid steps have been taken in enhancing its sports competitiveness. Public fitness activities and competitive sports are booming. The sport industry in Shandong demonstrates a strong momentum.

Photo by Pang Shouyi

在泰山之巅跨入新世纪

2000 年 1 月 1 日，3 万多人登顶泰山喜迎新千年到来，人们喜笑颜开、满怀期待。

这场声势浩大的"登泰山迎千年曙光"活动，通过全球 1000 多家卫星电视台向 138 个国家的 40 多亿观众进行滚动播出。"让我告诉世界，中国命运自己主宰……"当新千年的钟声响起、圣火被点燃，人们在《走进新时代》的歌声中迈向新世纪，美好的憧憬在每个人心中荡漾。走进新千年，中国各项事业的发展和人们的美好生活，翻开了历史的崭新篇章。

谷永威 摄

Greet the new millennium at the top of Mount Tai

On January 1, 2000, more than 30,000 people reach summit of Mount Tai in great excitement and anticipation to celebrate the arrival of the new millennium.

The event, with the theme of "Climb Mount Tai to Welcome the Dawn of the Millennium", was broadcasted live to more than 4 billion viewers in 138 countries through more than 1,000 satellite TV stations around the world. "Let me tell the world that, China is in control of her own destiny..." As the bell of the new millennium rang and the flame was lit, with the song *Walking into the New Era*, people entered into the new century with hearts full of bright hopes for the future. China entered a new chapter with the development of various undertakings and the happy life of people.

Photo by Gu Yongwei

火车来了

2003 年，沂蒙山区的老农坐看胶州—新沂铁路铺到家门口。

沂蒙山区不仅农业资源丰富，而且矿产资源丰富。但由于交通条件的限制，只能"捧着金碗要饭吃"。胶新铁路承担起了改写这段历史的重任。胶新铁路是"十五"期间国家铁路重点建设项目之一，2001 年12 月动工，2003 年 12 月全线投产运营。

铁路的开通，将沿线丰富的资源优势转化为经济优势，结束了鲁东南大部分市县不通铁路的历史，对沂蒙山区脱贫致富、经济腾飞产生了深远影响。

A new railway under construction

In 2003, old farmers in the Yimeng mountainous area sit and watch the Jiaozhou-Xinyi Railway being paved right at their doorstep.

Rich in agricultural and mineral resources but closed-off due to poor road infrastructure, Yimeng had long been "begging with a golden bowl". Jiaozhou-Xinyi Railway rewrote history for this area. The railway is one of the key national railway construction projects during the Tenth Five-Year Plan period. The construction started in December 2001, and the railway was open for use in December 2003.

The railway turned the abundant resources alongside the line into an economic advantage, and boosted poverty-alleviation and economic take-off in Yimeng region. The history of most cities and counties in southeastern Shandong not having railways was ended.

"当家人"，俺们自己选

2003 年 9 月 14 日，山东省首次社区居委会直接选举大会在济南市历下区甸柳第一小学举行。

这次居委会直选是在我国农村村民委员会直选普遍推广，城市社区居委会直选尚处在试点阶段的大背景下举行的。甸柳新村第一居委会是一个既有纯居民楼，又有机关、企事业单位宿舍楼的混合型社区，在济南市社区中具有代表性，成为山东省第一个实行直选试点的居委会。这是我国民主政治建设的一次新尝试和进步。

李霞 摄

Direct election held in a neighborhood community

On September 14, 2003, the first direct election of neighborhood committees in Shandong province is held at Dianliu No. 1 Primary School in Lixia District, Jinan.

The direct election of villagers committee was rolled out in a mass scale and that of neighborhood committees in cities was still a pilot program. The first neighborhood committee of Dianliu New Village covered an area where there were residential buildings and dormitory buildings of government departments, companies and public institutions, an epitome of many communities in Jinan. It became the first neighborhood committee to implement direct election in Shandong. This was a new attempt and progress in the development of political democracy in our country.

Photo by Li Xia

身边的榜样

2005 年 8 月 8 日，成百上千的人聚集在青岛崂山海岸边观看"麦莎"台风带来的海潮。一个巨浪袭来，把岸边的一位女青年卷入海中。见此情景，农民工魏青钢没有丝毫犹豫，纵身跳下两米多高的防浪墙，向落水女青年游去。跟巨浪搏斗了 40 多分钟，在民警的协助下，他终于把落水女子救上岸。

沧海横流，方显英雄本色。魏青钢和千千万万离乡离土的农民兄弟一样，奔波、忙碌，当他和我们擦肩而过时，也许并不被人注意，然而在救人的一瞬间，他已值得我们永远铭记。

钱程 摄

Rescue a woman swept away by waves

On August 8, 2005, hundreds of people gather on the coast of Mount Lao in Qingdao to watch the tides brought by Typhoon Matsa. A huge wave strikes and drags a young woman on the shore into the sea. Without a fractional hesitation, Wei Qinggang, a migrant worker, jumps off the two-meter-high seawall and swims to her rescue. Having fought against the tides for more than 40 minutes, he finally brings the drowning woman ashore with the help of the police.

Heroes often step forward in times of need. Wei Qinggang is one of the thousands of farmers who migrate to cities for a job, are busy making a living, and never get noticed. But from the moment he jumped into the sea, he is a hero imprinted in our memories.

Photo by Qian Cheng

"六姐妹"煎饼

　　蒙阴县烟庄村居住着共产党员"沂蒙六姐妹"，在革命战争时代，她们英勇支前，为子弟兵送军粮、做军鞋、看护伤病员，置自己的生命于不顾。她们是张玉梅、伊廷珍、杨桂英、伊淑英、冀贞兰、公方莲。

　　1947年6月10日，当时鲁中军区机关报《鲁中大众报》以"妇女支前拥军样样好"为题，报道了这支模范群体。从此，"沂蒙六姐妹"的名字传遍了整个沂蒙山区。迟浩田将军曾题词："沂蒙六姐妹，拥军情不忘"。2009年，一部以她们为原型的电影《沂蒙六姐妹》作为新中国成立60周年的献礼片，在全国公映，再一次感动了全国观众。

　　随着经济发展，当地企业注册了"六姐妹"品牌煎饼，聘请五位老人做了名誉厂长，并为她们印制了名片。能为自己的家乡办点事情，她们很开心。

　　沂蒙老区这片热土，哺育了英雄的人民。斯人已故，精神永在。

王忠家　摄

Six old ladies who assisted war efforts when they were young

In the Yanzhuang Village of Mengyin County, there were the "Six Yimeng Sisters", who were the Party members. During the wars, they risked their lives and made courageous moves to support the soldiers. They delivered food and made shoes for soldiers, and looked after the wounded and sick. These heroes are Zhang Yumei, Yi Tingzhen, Yang Guiying, Yi Shuying, Ji Zhenlan, and Gong Fanglian.

On June 10, 1947, the then *Luzhong Dazhong Daily*, the official newspaper of Luzhong military region, published an article titled "Great Women Supporting the Army", praising the good deeds of this model group. From that time, the name of the "Six Yimeng Sisters" was spread throughout the Yimeng mountainous area. General Chi Haotian once wrote an inscription, "The military will never forget the six Yimeng sisters." In 2009, a film featuring their story, *The Six Sisters of Yimeng*, was released nationwide to celebrate the 60th anniversary of new China, which moved the audiences around the country once again.

With the economic development, a local pancake company registered the brand name of "Six Sisters", and hired the five of them to be their honorary directors and made business cards for them. The sisters were very happy that they could do something for their hometown.

As an old revolutionary base area, Yimeng has nurtured heroic people. The heroes are long gone, but their heroic spirit will carry on.

Photo by Wang Zhongjia

欢乐颂

2006 年 7 月 7 日，中国济南首届国际儿童联欢节开幕。

这是济南市政府全力打造的精品节庆，活动采取政府主导、各界参与的方式，为孩子们准备了一桌丰盛、有趣的文化大餐。来自 16 个国家和地区的 200 多名少年代表参加此次盛会。活动主题为"同一蓝天，欢乐童年"，3 天的时间内，各国儿童游览济南名胜，学习民俗制作，共植友谊树，观看航模表演，制作"我们的左右手"国际儿童手模友谊墙，启动水地球，发布环保和节水宣言，举行一系列精彩纷呈的联欢活动。

高玉琦 摄

Joyous kids from both China and overseas

On July 7, 2006, the first International Children's Festival in Jinan is held.

Led by the government of Jinan and joined by people from all walks of life, the three-day festival was a cultural event featuring interesting activities, with over 200 children from 16 countries and regions participating, themed on "A Happy Childhood under the Same Sky". During the event, children toured various destinations in Jinan, learned how to make folk art crafts, planted trees together to symbolize friendship, watched airplane model performance, painted their hands on a friendship wall named "Our Left and Right Hands", activated a water globe and issued a declaration to protect the environment and conserve water.

Photo by Gao Yuqi

爱的力量

2008年5月12日，以北纬31度、东经103.4度为中心，相当于数百颗原子弹的能量，在10万平方公里的区域释放。霎时间，山崩地裂，江河呜咽。北京、重庆、湖南、湖北、陕西、山西、河北、山东等近半个中国有震感。

灾难发生后，山东各方力量紧急集结，千里驰援四川。山东人用实际行动践行着山东精神，传播着齐鲁大爱。

救援队在废墟上忙碌、穿梭，他们在抗震救灾现场百折不挠、舍身忘我，用"不抛弃，不放弃"的信念谱写了爱的壮美诗篇。

Rush to rescue earthquake victims in Sichuan

On May 12, 2008, an earthquake with the energy impact of several hundred atomic bombs happened at 31 degrees north latitude and 103.4 degrees east longitude, sweeping an area of 100,000 square kilometers. In a single moment, the earth shakes, the ground cracks, and the rivers tremble. Nearly half of China, including Beijing, Chongqing, Hunan, Hubei, Shaanxi, Shanxi, Hebei, and Shandong, feel the earthquake.

After the disaster, Shandong gathered strength and rushed to Sichuan's aid, demonstrating the Shandong spirit of great compassion with actual action.

The rescue team rushed in and out of the ruins with true resilience and selflessness at the earthquake relief site. With the belief of never giving up, they had written heroic epics of love and compassion.

直挂云帆济沧海

　　2008 年 8 月 9 日至 8 月 23 日，第二十九届奥运会帆船比赛在青岛奥林匹克帆船中心举行。

　　中国帆船队获金牌、铜牌各 1 枚，实现中国帆船项目奥运金牌零的突破。青岛奥帆赛首次设立奖牌轮和胜利者返航线，在海上平台进行颁奖，创造了"青岛模式"。伴随着 2008 年北京奥运会的成功举办，作为协办城市的青岛，不但圆满完成了奥运任务，也把帆船之都的名号传向了世界。

周青先 摄

Olympic Sailing competition held in Qingdao

From August 9 to August 23, 2008, the Sailing Regatta of the 29th Olympic Games is held at the Qingdao Olympic Sailing Center.

The Chinese sailing team won one gold medal and one bronze, the first ever gold medal in this sport. For the first time, the competition introduced a medal race at the sailing games and a return route for the winners with the award ceremony at an offshore platform, creating the "Qingdao Model". As the co-host city of the successful 2008 Beijing Olympic Games, Qingdao accomplished its mission and earned the reputation as a sailing capital.

Photo by Zhou Qingxian

俺家买了小轿车

滨州农民喜提自己梦寐以求的轿车。

随着农村经济的发展，农民收入提高，生产生活方式悄然发生改变，不断产生新的消费理念，在衣食住行方面有了更高的追求，小轿车成为广大农民群众的新宠。

We have just bought a car

Farmers in Binzhou buy their own cars.

As the rural economy developed and farmer's income increased, their production style, lifestyle and consumption style have also changed. They wanted better things in life and buying cars became a trend.

济南欢迎您

金秋时节，硕果累累。2009 年 10 月，第十一届全运会在山东省举行。

在筹办第十一届全运会的四年多时间里，山东省秉持"开放办全运、创新办全运、节俭办全运、文明办全运"的思路，为全运会搭建了新的广阔舞台。举办赛事的各个城市高度重视开发体育赛事的综合功能，统筹谋划，精心布局，为将全运会打造成集体育、经济、文化、环境等为一体的大型公众活动做了充分准备。

第十一届全运会成为展现山东人民奋发进取精神风貌的窗口，也对经济社会发展起到有力的推动作用。

李霞 摄

National sports meeting held in Jinan, capital city of Shandong

In the golden season of autumn, the 11th National Games is held in Shandong in October 2009.

Shandong had been preparing for the games for four years with the idea of "openness, innovation, frugality and courtesy", putting in place a stage for successful games. Every host city attached great importance to tapping into comprehensive functions of sports, and made thorough plans to turn this game into a large public sport event integrating sports, economy, culture, and environmental protection.

The 11th National Games became a window to show the enterprising spirit of Shandong people. It also played a significant role in promoting economic and social development.

Photo by Li Xia

大片来了

自 2007 年中国第一家 IMAX 影城在东莞落户以来，7 年间中国就拥有了 100 多块 IMAX 银幕，IMAX 在中国的发展迎来黄金时期。2010 年山东第一家 IMAX 影院开业，到影院看电影的群众可以享受到超大屏幕带来的视听盛宴。

2018 年，山东省印发《山东省影视产业发展规划（2018—2022 年）》，从影视园区、精品生产、机构主体、市场拓展等方面，对今后五年山东影视产业发展作出了全面系统的规划布局，提出要持续改善影视创作营商投资环境，大幅提升国际优秀影视企业市场准入的开放度、透明度。

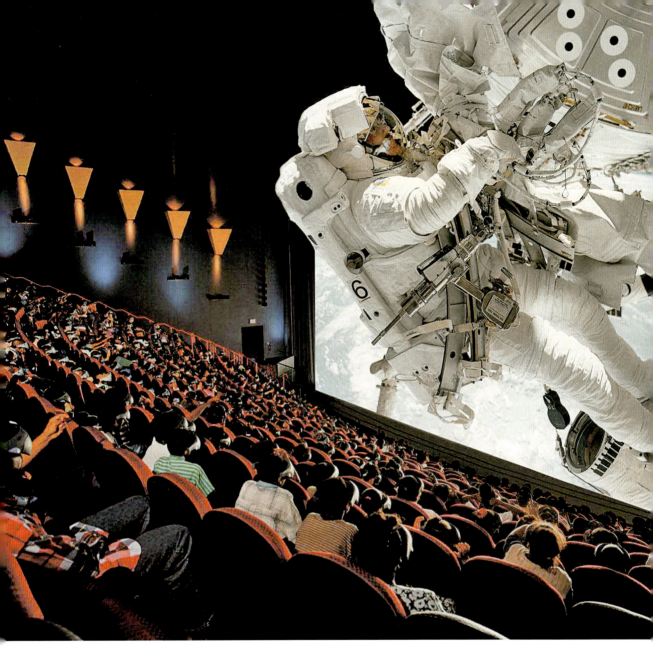

The first IMAX movie theater in Shandong

Since the first IMAX cinema in China opened in Dongguan in 2007, over 100 IMAX screens had been put up within 7 years, ushering in its golden age in the country. In 2010, Shandong had its first IMAX cinema, where audience can enjoy films with extra-large screens.

In 2018, Shandong issued *Shandong Film and Television Industry development Plan (2018—2022)*, a systematic blueprint for the development of the film and television industry for the next 5 years, covering theme parks, quality production, business entities and market expansion. This plan has proposed to continuously improve the industrial environment, business operation and related investments and ensure far more open and transparent market access for top-notch international companies in this industry.

打开博物馆之门

山东博物馆于 2010 年迎来新馆建成开馆，前来参观的市民络绎不绝。

进入新世纪以来，山东省的社会经济快速发展，人民生活水平不断提升，对文化设施和文化生活提出了更高要求。2006 年，山东省委省政府提出了建设山东文化强省的战略目标，山东省博物馆新馆建设又一次提上日程，成为省委省政府贯彻落实科学发展观，繁荣发展山东文化事业，促进文化资源大省向文化强省跨越的一项重大决策。新馆选址在济南市区主干道经十路东段，2007 年 12 月 29 日奠基，2010 年 6 月竣工，2010 年 11 月 16 日正式向社会开放，山东省博物馆至此更名山东博物馆，开启了文博事业新篇章，也成为正在崛起中的省会城市文博休闲圈的地标性建筑。

山东博物馆自建成以后，免费向市民开放，市民可以通过有效身份证件换取门票进行参观，博物馆已经成为越来越多的市民游客体验文化、学习历史、互动交流的场所。作为宣传齐鲁文化的重要窗口，山东博物馆依托各类展览和推广形式多样的社会教育活动，极大丰富了人民的精神文化生活，满足了人民对文化生活的需要。

刘亚中 摄

The new Shandong Museum

The new Shandong Museum, opened in 2010, greets a lot of visitors.

Since the beginning of the new century, in the context of the rapid social and economic development and steady improvement in living standards, people's demands for cultural facilities and a better cultural life have grown. In 2006, the CPC Shandong Provincial Committee and Shandong Provincial Government proposed the strategic goal of building a strong cultural province, and put the construction of the Shandong Provincial Museum on the agenda. It was a major decision to implement the Scientific Outlook on Development, promote cultural prosperity, and transform Shandong from a province endowed with cultural resources to a culture powerhouse. The new museum is located in the east section of Jingshi Road, the main road in Jinan. The foundation stone was laid on December 29, 2007. It was completed in June 2010 and officially opened to the public on November 16, 2010 under the new name Shandong Museum. It became a landmark and opened a new chapter for cultural exhibitions in the provincial capital.

Since the establishment of the museum, citizens can obtain free tickets after verification of their ID cards. More and more people come and experience culture, learn history, and interact with each other. As an important window for people to have a glance at the Qilu culture, Shandong Museum has held various exhibitions and promoted diverse educational activities, enriching the intellectual and cultural life of our people.

Photo by Liu Yazhong

高铁时代来临

2011 年 6 月 30 日下午 4 点 48 分，济南西站顺利迎来京沪高铁首发列车 G1。

它是济南西站乃至齐鲁大地迎来的第一趟正式运营的高速旅客列车，标志着作为京沪高铁五大始发站之一的济南西站正式建成启用，也标志着山东正式进入"高铁时代"。

十八大以来，山东铁路建设真正驶上快车道。京沪高铁、青荣城际、石济高铁、德大铁路、龙烟铁路等新线陆续建成通车，山东融入全国高铁网。鲁南高铁、郑济高铁、济莱城际等相继开工建设，2018 年底，济青高铁、青连铁路建成通车。截至 2020 年底，山东全省开通运营的高铁里程超 2100 公里，位列全国第三。

The era of high-speed railway has arrived

At 4:48 p.m. on June 30, 2011, G1, the first high-speed train from Beijing to Shanghai, arrives in Jinan West Railway Station.

It was the first high-speed train that officially arrived in Jinan West Railway Station and the first in the entire Shandong Province. As one of the five major departure stations alongside the Beijing-Shanghai High-speed Railway line, Jinan West Railway Station was now officially in use, ushering Shandong into the era of "high-speed railway".

Since the 18th National Congress of the CPC, Shandong railway construction has been developing rapidly. New lines such as Beijing-Shanghai High-speed Railway, Qingdao-Rongcheng Intercity Railway, Shijiazhuang-Jinan High-speed Railway, Dezhou-Dajiawa Railway and Longkou-Yantai Railway have been completed and opened for use, integrating Shandong into the national high-speed railway network. Construction of the South Shandong High-speed Railway, Zhengzhou-Jinan High-speed Railway, and Jinan-Laiwu Intercity Railway started one after another. At the end of 2018, the Jinan-Qingdao High-speed Railway and Qingdao-Lianyungang Railway were completed and started operation. As of the end of 2020, Shandong registered a mileage of 2,100 kilometers of high-speed railway in operation, ranking third in the country.

希望的田野　A Land of Promise

俺们的手艺进京了

　　2011 年 1 月 9 日，"手艺农村——山东农村文化产业调研成果展"在中国美术馆举办。展览历时 10 天，围绕手艺主题，集 4000 余件手艺产品，通过文献及实物、手艺人演示、手艺创意和学术研讨会的形式，对山东省潍坊、临沂、菏泽 3 市的 7 项手工文化进行展示，涉及潍坊杨家埠木版年画、风筝，临沂柳编，红花乡中国结，曹县桐杨木艺，鄄城土布，巨野农民工笔绘画等，包含了产业发展、理论研究、设计创意等，生动展示了山东农村文化产业发展成果。

　　山东是传统手工艺大省，具有丰富的手工技艺资源和良好的产业基础，这些传统手艺将农村丰富的劳动力转化为生产力，促进了农民增收致富。

李楠 摄

Shandong rural handcrafts on exhibition in Beijing

On January 9, 2011, "Handicraft in Shandong's Countryside" is held at the National Art Museum of China.

The ten-day event exhibited over 4,000 handicraft items through various literature, artifacts, live demonstration and academic workshops. 7 types of handicraft culture from Weifang, Linyi and Heze were also displayed, such as Weifang Yangjiabu New Year paintings, Weifang kites, Linyi willow wickerwork, Honghua Chinese knots, Caoxian wood artwork, Juancheng homespun, and traditional paintings by farmers in Juye, covering industrial development, theoretical study and design, and demonstrating accomplishments of rural cultural sector in Shandong.

Shandong is known for traditional handicrafts as evidenced by an abundant resource of skills and a solid industrial foundation. These traditional skills have transformed the rich labor force in the countryside into productivity and increased farmers' income and wealth.

Photo by Li Nan

青春正是读书时

2012 年，济南皇亭体育馆，准备考研的大学生们在听课。

2013 年，山东 172308 名考生参加硕士研究生入学考试，同比增长 7.9%，再创历史新高。

莘莘学子，追求知识，为美好的未来不懈努力。为了满足广大学子接受高等教育的渴求，山东不断推进高等教育改革，建设研究生教育优质课堂，建设研究生教育联合培养基地和德学双馨的师资队伍，加强国际交流合作，扩大研究生教育开放度，为研究生教育创造了良好的环境，使研究生教育成为拔尖创新人才的摇篮。

于泽 摄

Mass tutoring class given in a gymnasium to students for master's degrees

In 2012, in Jinan Huangting Gymnasium, college students preparing for the postgraduate entrance examination attend classes.

In 2013, 172,308 candidates from Shandong took the entrance examination of graduate schools, an increase of 7.9%, setting a record high.

Numerous students work tirelessly in the pursuit of knowledge and a better future. In order to satisfy students' thirst for higher education, Shandong has promoted higher education reforms. It has introduced quality graduate education classes, built a joint education base for masters' candidates, and fostered excellent professional faculties with high moral integrity. The province has also strengthened international exchanges and cooperation, and expanded the accessibility of graduate education. As a result, a nurturing environment has been created for graduate education that produces top-notch innovative talents.

Photo by Yu Ze

"四德"润乡风

2012 年 5 月，东营市六户镇神堂村，"好媳妇""好婆婆"评选表彰大会现场。村民们你一言、我一语，喜笑颜开。

为了重塑"礼仪之邦"的道德高地，山东自 2007 年起，启动实施"四德工程"。家庭美德突出"孝德"，职业道德突出"诚德"，社会公德突出"爱德"，个人品德突出"仁德"。公民道德规范具体化、生活化，说的是群众贴心入耳的话，树的是群众触手可及的杆，让善行义举上榜，为凡人善举立传。

Ladies who are cited for fostering rural ethnics

In May 2012, in Shentang Village, Liuhu Town, Dongying, villagers smile and chat at the "Good Wife" and "Good Mother-in-law" selection and commendation ceremony.

In order to encourage morality, Shandong initiated the "Four Virtues Project" in 2007, advocating "filial piety" in family life, "honesty" in professional ethics, "charity" in social life, and "benevolence" as personal virtue. These moral norms were interpreted into concrete things people can do in daily life. The language was colloquial to better help people understand, and practical and achievable standards were set. Good deeds would be publicized, and good people would be written into biographies.

"大鼻子"校车进山啦

2012年，山东省沂源县山里娃坐上平安车。

往年，不少学生上学需要家长每天用自行车、三轮车等交通工具接送，还有一些私人运营公司用淘汰的旧车接送学生，存在严重的安全隐患。近年来，山东省多地把解决学生上下学"乘车难"问题列入民生工程，加大财政投入，购置符合国家安全标准的校车，并严格规范校车安全管理，切实保证校车行驶安全。

School buses come to mountain village

    In 2012, in Yiyuan County, Shandong, the kids board a school bus.

    In previous years, students were dropped off and picked up from school by their parents' bikes and tricycles, or by obsolete cars owned by small private companies, posing serious safety problems. In recent years, Shandong has increased fiscal inputs to solve the commuting problem of students, and listed it as an official project to improve people's livelihood. Localities in the province have purchased school buses that meet national safety standards, and formulated strict regulations to ensure school bus safety.

奋斗的幸福

Happiness Earned Through Hard Work

"达·芬奇"来了

2013 年 10 月 9 日，达·芬奇《自画像》在山东博物馆与观众见面，这幅举世闻名的画作也是首次来中国展出。同它一道而来的还有毕加索、达利、伦勃朗、雷诺阿、戈雅等艺术大师的 353 件绘画、雕塑和陶瓷作品。

此次欧洲经典美术作品大展，无论从展品数量还是从展品质量看，都堪称国际"重磅级"艺术盛宴。大展分为"文艺复兴时期艺术大师经典原作展""欧洲现代艺术大师经典原作展""当代艺术大师经典原作展"，以点带面，将西方艺术发展脉络呈现给观众。

张健 摄

Self-portrait of Leonardo da Vinci on exhibition in Shandong Museum

The *Self Portrait* by Leonardo da Vinci is exhibited in Shandong Museum on October 9, 2013, marking the debut in China of this world-famous painting. What are exhibited together include 353 paintings, sculptures and ceramic works of Picasso, Dali, Rembrandt, Renoir, Goya and other artists.

Judged from the quantity and quality of exhibits, this European classic artwork exhibition was a grand gathering of international masterpieces. Composed of "Exhibition of Classic Original Works of Renaissance Masters", "Exhibition of Classic Original Works of European Modern Masters" and "Exhibition of Classic Original Works of Contemporary Masters", the exhibition showcased the evolution of western art by bringing together works in different periods.

Photo by Zhang Jian

亭台楼阁　曲山艺海

2013年9月，济南趵突泉公园白雪楼戏台正在上演戏曲《小姑贤》。

每逢周末，趵突泉公园白雪楼戏台都有戏曲演出，节假日，这里更是好戏连台，京剧、吕剧、山东梆子，连续登场，票友们在这里大饱耳福。

2019年9月，全国非遗曲艺周系列活动在济南举行，国内代表性非遗曲艺项目和传承人齐聚济南，他们分别在黑虎泉公园、百花洲历史文化街区里的百花洲剧场、趵突泉公园白雪楼戏台，表演老百姓喜闻乐见的剧目，深受欢迎。

程永林　摄

A local opera performed on traditional pavilion stage

In September 2013, the traditional Chinese opera *Sister-in-Law* is performed at Baixue Pavilion in Baotu Spring Park.

There are traditional Chinese opera performances at Baixue Pavilion in Baotu Spring Park every weekend, and more brilliant performances are put on one after another during holidays. Here fans can enjoy Peking Opera, Lü Opera and Shandong Bangzi (Wooden Clapper Opera).

The China Intangible Cultural Heritage Folk Art Week was held in Jinan in September 2019, attracting representative intangible cultural heritage art forms and inheritors from all over the country. Artists performed popular dramas in Black Tiger Spring Park, Baihua Pond Theatre of the Baihua Pond Historical and Cultural Street and Baixue Pavilion in Baotu Spring Park, which were warmly welcomed by the general public.

Photo by Cheng Yonglin

小菜篮，大民生

2013 年，寿光市洛城街道东斟灌村彩椒丰收。

多年来，山东省瓜菜产业凭借标准化、产业化、国际化的鲜明特点，确保人民的"菜篮子"品类丰富，质量安全。

生产方面，山东率先提出"发展高产、优质、高效农业"口号，全面推行农业标准化生产，在育苗、移栽、施肥、用药等环节实现了标准化生产，从田间到餐桌实行全程监控，织就了一张农产品质量安全大网。产业链延伸方面，山东结合农村经济结构战略性调整，提出产业化发展模式，引导农民开展种植、加工、运输、销售一条龙服务，保障了人民群众"菜蓝子"供应。

韩明云 摄

Abundant supply of vegetables

Color pepper registers a bumpy harvest in Dongzhenguan Village, Luocheng Sub-district, Shouguang City in 2013.

For years, Shandong has ensured the supply of different kinds of quality vegetables with its standardized, industrialized and international melon and vegetable sectors.

As the first province to put forward the vision to develop high-yield, fine-quality and high-efficient agriculture, Shandong has fully advanced standardized agricultural production, covering seedling cultivation, transplanting, fertilization and insecticide application. THe whole-process monitoring from fields to dinner tables forms a safety net to ensure the quality of farm produce. Shandong has also worked to extend its agricultural industrial chain. Guided by strategic restructuring of rural economy, Shandong has developed a mode of agricultural industrialization. Farmers are encouraged to provide one-stop services, covering planting, processing, transportation and marketing, in an effort to ensure vegetable supply for the public.

Photo by Han Mingyun

老爷爷的"新宠"

2013 年，自从子女给买了智能手机，耄耋之年的老爷爷"机"不离手，照看重孙之余，也让孩子教着玩微信、下象棋。

随着移动互联网技术的普及，农民的生活发生了巨大变化，这得益于智能手机的广泛应用，下至儿童、上至老人，都开始热衷使用智能手机，村里建起了微信群，村民一起商讨大事，网上购物、网络直播带货……科技创新、无远弗届，信息技术为农村打通了与外界的广泛交流联系，带动了广大农民开启新生活新风尚，从日常生活到文化建设，从社群交流到娱乐游戏都有了新的故事。

宁舟浩 摄

Grandpa's new favorite item

The 80-plus-year-old grandpa has his new personal favorite, a smart-phone as a gift from his children, in 2013. Helping take care of his great grandson, he is happy to have little children teach him to use WeChat and play Chinese chess on the phone.

The wide application of mobile Internet technology and high penetration rate of smart-phones have brought great changes to the life of rural residents. From senior people to children, smart-phones are becoming popular. They discuss village affairs in WeChat groups, go online shopping and sell products through live streaming. Technological innovation transcends geographical barriers and IT technology creates a new lifestyle in rural areas by enabling extensive exchanges with the outside world. There are new stories to tell from daily life to cultural development and from community engagement to entertainment.

Photo by Ning Zhouhao

"鸢都"嘉年华

　　2014年4月潍坊风筝节，世界各地的爱好者在此放飞纸鸢。

　　"草长莺飞二月天，拂堤杨柳醉春烟。儿童散学归来早，忙趁东风放纸鸢。""纸鸢"就是风筝，历史悠久，自古至今"放纸鸢"都是充满生活情趣的乐事。潍坊是风筝的故乡，被誉为"鸢都"，制作风筝的技艺源远流长，传承至今，是我国弥足珍贵的手工艺，被评为国家级非物质文化遗产。

　　1984年4月1日，首届潍坊国际风筝节盛大开幕，来自世界各地的个人和团体参加了此次盛会，盛况空前，在国内外引起广泛关注。从此潍坊风筝节阔步前进，每年都按时举办，每年都亮点纷呈，成为世界了解潍坊的一扇窗口，也使潍坊走向世界，大大促进了当地经济和旅游业的发展。近年来，为了更好地发挥风筝节的带动作用，节会期间，还同时举办鲁台贸洽会、寿光菜博会、潍坊工业产品展销会、昌乐珠宝展销订货会、临朐奇石展销会等经贸活动，为风筝节注入新的活力。

张景国 摄

Carnival in Weifang, Capital of Kites

Fans from all over the world are flying kites during the Weifang International Kite Festival in April, 2014.

As a poem in the Qing Dynasty goes, "February sees grass grow and thrushes fly; over banks willows flick and spring mist high. After-school kids come home early, keen to fly paper birds while East Wind is spry." Paper bird in this poem refers to kites. Since ancient times, to fly kites has always been an activity full of joy. Weifang, home of kites, is a renowned Capital of Kites. The time-honored kite-making technique has been passed down to this day. As a valuable handicraft in China, it has been recognized as National Intangible Cultural Heritage.

The grand opening of the first Weifang International Kite Festival fell on April 1, 1984, attracting global attention and the participation of individuals and groups across the world. Since then, the Weifang International Kite Festival, as a yearly event, has seen rapid development and highlights in each gathering. As an opportunity through which the world gets to know more about Weifang and the Weifang embraces the world, it has significantly boosted the development of local economy and tourism. In recent years, to better leverage the festival, business and trade events such as Shandong-Taiwan Economic and Trade Fair, China (Shouguang) International Vegetable Science and Technology Fair, Weifang Industrial Products Trade Fair, Changle Jewellery Trade Fair and Linqu Rare Stone Trade Fair have also been held during the kite festival, injecting new vitality to the event.

Photo by Zhang Jingguo

俺们也能学 3D

沂水县实验中学的学生正在崭新的微机室学习 3D 打印技术。

3D 打印技术，可在短时间、简工艺程序下制作出结构复杂、尺寸精细、性能特殊的艺术模型、零部件等，所以它被广泛应用在工业制造、生物医疗、建筑工程、科学研究等领域中。3D 打印课进校园将使得学生在创新能力和动手实践能力上得到训练。

3D 打印课在乡村学校的开设，让乡村孩子们可以与城市孩子一样享受优质的教育资源。

3D-printing taught in a rural school

Students in Experimental Middle School of Yishui County study 3D printing technology in the brand-new computer room.

With 3D printing, complicated, delicate and special-purpose art models and components can be made through simple procedures in a short period of time. It is therefore widely used in such areas as manufacturing, biomedicine, constructional engineering and scientific research. 3D printing courses can inspire students to innovate and offer more hands-on opportunities.

The availability of 3D printing courses in rural schools enable rural students to access high-quality education resources as their urban peers do.

书香曲水亭

　　2015 年 7 月，曲水亭街旁，游客小憩。

　　这种画面最容易让人想起卞之琳的这首诗："你站在桥上看风景，看风景的人在楼上看你，明月装饰了你的窗子，你装饰了别人的梦。"在济南，这种诗意画面随处可见。

　　千百年来，在泉水的浸润下，泉城济南生动明丽。2017 年，济南举全城之力，凝心聚力，创建全国文明城市。大力完善城市基础设施，拆除违规建筑，绿化美化环境，鼓励文明出行，加大志愿者服务力度，厚植城市文明素养，让泉城水更清，山更绿，天空更蓝，人民群众的幸福感、获得感更强烈，幸福美好成为城市的底色。

张平 摄

Leisure reading by the stream

A tourist rests at Qushuiting Street in July, 2015.

Such a scene easily reminds us of a poem by Bian Zhilin, which goes "When you watch the scenery from the bridge, the sightseer watches you from the balcony. The bright moon adorns your window, while you adorn another's dream." Such a poetic scene is commonly seen in Jinan.

For thousands of years, the lively and bright city of Jinan is nourished by springs. In 2017, Jinan went all out to build itself into a National City of Civic Virtue. Enormous efforts were made to improve urban infrastructure, demolish unapproved construction projects, upgrade city environment, urge citizens to abide by traffic rules, step up volunteer service and build up civic virtue of the city. These steps have turned Jinan into a city with clearer waters, greener mountains and a clearer sky, and created a stronger sense of gain and fulfillment for local residents. Happiness has become the most salient feature of Jinan.

Photo by Zhang Ping

海上"良田"

2015 年 7 月，烟台大型海洋牧场中设置的海上网箱。

瀚海碧波中，海洋牧场的建设运营，正在悄然改变传统渔业生产方式，创造出更多的可能性。

海洋牧场是基于海洋生态学原理和现代海洋工程技术，充分利用自然生产力，在特定海域科学培育和管理渔业资源的人工渔场。近岸海域连片养殖和粗放的饵料投喂，是渔业养殖的主要方式，它的特点是产出大，污染大，周而复始，"鱼"越养越小。如今，在现代化海洋牧场的带动下，渔业养殖从近海走向远海，从粗放转为精细，拥有了科学的养殖方式和广袤的发展空间，海上"良田"越来越肥沃。

Cage culture

The picture shows net cages in a large marine ranch in Yantai in July, 2015.

The construction and operation of marine ranch in the vast ocean is gradually changing traditional fishery, creating more possibilities.

Marine ranch refers to human-operated fishing grounds that develop and manage fishing resources at certain waters by relying on marine ecological principles and modern maritime engineering technologies, and fully leveraging the productive force of nature. Traditional fishery approach was concentrated on breeding and extensive feeding in offshore areas, which produced high yield but also severe pollution, resulting in dwindling fishery resources. Driven by modern marine ranch technologies, fishing grounds have gone from offshore areas to high seas and from extensive management to intensive management. With science-based breeding techniques and broad prospects, the marine ranch is unleashing more and more potential.

留住乡愁

2015 年 11 月，临清市近古村建起村史馆。

一张张老照片见证一段段难忘的岁月，一行行文字记载了乡村的发展变迁史。村史馆是"记得住乡愁"的重要载体，它融合了一般意义上档案馆、博物馆等文化设施的某些特点与功能，同时又具有独立性。在收藏与展陈、教育与娱乐、保存与传承、乡村治理等方面具有重要价值。

村史馆通过展示村庄的发展变迁，将乡土文化细致展现，守住了文明之根。

张健 摄

Exhibition of village history

An exhibition hall of village history is set up in Jingu Village of Linqing City in November, 2015.

The old photos have witnessed many indelible moments and lines of words demonstrate the history of rural development and changes. The exhibition hall is an important platform to preserve tradition in the rural area. It integrates features of archives and museums, and also has its own characteristics. It is of great value in terms of collection, display, education, entertainment, preservation, inheriting and rural governance.

By exhibiting the development and changes of the village, the exhibition hall demonstrates traditional rural culture and preserves the cultural root.

Photo by Zhang Jian

淘出幸福路

2016 年 5 月 24 日，在济南章丘三德范村的电子商务服务中心，村里不识字的妇女，正在挑选自己喜爱的衣服，专职淘宝员帮助她们下单购买。

2016 年 3 月，齐鲁"互联网+"示范基地暨阿里村淘宝服务中心正式运营。作为阿里巴巴在济南市的第一家农村淘宝运营中心，章丘农村淘宝项目是章丘与阿里巴巴深度合作的基础和平台，通过搭建市、镇、村三级电商服务网络，实现"网货下乡"和"农产品进城"的双向流通，并能带动章丘青年创业、就业，激活农村电子商务生态，促进农村经济发展。

王剑 摄

Online shopping in a rural village

On May 24, 2016, illiterate women villagers are picking clothes they favor on Taobao, an e-commerce platform in China, with the help of an online shopping guide in the e-commerce service center in Sandefan Village, Zhangqiu District of Jinan City.

The Alibaba Taobao service center, also an "Internet Plus" demonstration base, was officially put into operation in March, 2016. As Alibaba's first Taobao operation center in rural areas in Jinan, the project was the foundation and platform of close cooperation between Zhangqiu and Alibaba. By establishing a three-tier e-commerce service network at city, town and village levels, it has helped online goods enter rural market and rural products enter urban market, facilitated business startup initiatives and employment of the young people, energized the e-commerce in rural areas and promoted rural economy.

Photo by Wang Jian

高铁速度

2015 年 12 月 24 日，济青高铁全线开工，2018 年 12 月 26 日建成并通车运营。

济青高速铁路，是中国第一条以地方为主投资建设的高速铁路，是中国"四纵四横"快速铁路网青太客运通道的重要组成部分。从济南到青岛最快仅需 1 小时 40 分钟，城市与城市之间加速融合，城市之间渐无分野。

该高速铁路贯穿山东半岛，自济南东站引出，经邹平、淄博、青州、潍坊、高密、胶州，引入青岛铁路枢纽红岛站。沿途设济南东站、章丘北站、邹平站、淄博北站、临淄北站、青州北站、潍坊北站、高密北站、胶州北站、青岛机场站、红岛站共 11 站，正线全长 307.9 公里，构筑起山东省"三纵三横"城际轨道交通网主通道。

以济南、青岛两座区域中心城市为起点，便捷、快速、安全、高效、环保的高速轨道交通网络逐步成型。

郭尧 摄

Laying tracks of a high-speed railway

Jinan-Qingdao High-speed Railway starts construction on December 24, 2015 and is put into operation on December 26, 2018.

Jinan-Qingdao High-speed Railway is the first high-speed railway invested mainly by local funding. It is an indispensable part of the Qingdao-Taiyuan passenger transport corridor, which is one of the eight backbones constituting the high-speed railway network in China. After its completion, it only takes 1 hour and 40 minutes to travel from Jinan to Qingdao. As a result, distance of cities has been shortened and boundaries blurred.

The railway travels across Shandong peninsula, starting from Jinan East Station, passing by Zouping, Zibo, Qingzhou, Weifang, Gaomi, Jiaozhou and stopping at Hongdao Station, a railway hub in Qingdao. Along the 307.9 kilometers, there are 11 stations, namely Jinan East Station, Zhangqiu North Station, Zouping Station, Zibo North Station, Linzi North Station, Qingzhou North Station, Weifang North Station, Gaomi North Station, Jiaozhou North Station, Qingdao Airport Station and Hongdao Station. It is one of the major lines in the six backbone inter-city railways in Shandong.

An accessible, speedy, safe, efficient and environment-friendly high-speed railway network starting from two regional centers, namely Jinan and Qingdao, is gradually taking shape.

Photo by Guo Yao

恩爱就要"秀"出来

2016年9月，一对年轻人在秀恩爱。现在年轻人喜欢"秀恩爱"，在社交媒体上大方地将自己的幸福"秀"出来。

Record this happy occasion of wedding

A young couple is taking a photo in September 2016. Young people like to show they are in love on social media as a display of happiness.

俺也进车间了

2016 年 11 月，菏泽鄄城服装加工扶贫车间内，当地村民正在忙着工作。

菏泽市鄄城县立足户外家具、纺织服装、发制品产业优势，引导企业把加工车间建在村里，吸引贫困群众、留守妇女到车间打工，被群众称为"扶贫车间"。通过这种方式，不仅实现了贫困人口就地就近就业，让他们挣钱照顾家两不误，而且提升了乡村文明和村级治理水平，促进了农村和谐发展。

2017 年 2 月，"扶贫车间"被纳入中央政治局第 39 次集体学习的精准扶贫案例之一。

杨超 摄

Workshop in village helps raise rural income

A local villager is busy making clothes in a poverty-reduction workshop in Juancheng County of Heze City in November, 2016.

Relying on its industrial advantages in outdoor furniture, textile and garment, and hairwork, Juancheng County encouraged enterprises to set up workshops in villages to meet the employment need of impoverished villagers and stay-at-home women. These workshops, known among locals as poverty-reduction workshops, have ensured jobs near homes for impoverished villagers, allowing them to earn a living while looking after their families, and stepped up rural civility and village governance, promoting harmonious development in rural areas.

The poverty-reduction workshop was included among cases of precision poverty reduction for the 39th group study of the Political Bureau of the CPC Central Committee in February, 2017.

Photo by Yang Chao

奶奶发红包了

2017 年 2 月 17 日，春节。在平度市大泽山镇桑杭村，曹建伟一家欢聚在一起，老奶奶用手机微信给儿孙们发新年红包，大家乐成一团。

这只是一个普通农村家庭的欢乐瞬间，却是齐鲁大地上成千上万个幸福家庭的缩影。

刘惟青 摄

Grandma shares her joy with family during Spring Festival

Cao Jianwei and his families get together in Sanghang Village, Dazeshan Town, Pingdu City, during the Spring Festival on February 17 in 2017. In jolly festivity, Grandma sends red packets to her grandchildren through WeChat.

This joyful moment of a common rural family represents tens of thousands of happy families in Shandong.

Photo by Liu Weiqin

一家人的小日子

临朐县九山镇牛寨村村民沈祥强一家在老房子前合影。这一年，一场大病夺去了沈祥强父亲的生命，巨额医药费让这个家庭陷入了困境，家庭的重担落在沈祥强身上。

2017年5月，沈祥强一家5口人、5辆车在新居前合影。沈祥强在村里承包了一个苹果园、一个桃园，还有10亩地。农忙时他在家种地，农闲时外出打工，年收入4万多元。

牛寨村坐落在深山之中，偏僻冷清，生态良好，自然资源丰富。依托得天独厚的自然资源，当地大力发展生态旅游，打造乡村旅游样板，激活当地农业，使当地百姓增加了收入，过上了幸福生活，沈祥强家便是其中一户代表。

张健 摄

How life has changed on this family

The first picture is about Shen Xiangqiang and his family in front of his old house in Niuzhai Village, Jiushan Town, Linqu County. In the same year, his father died of a serious disease. The huge medical cost reduced this family to financial difficulties and the heavy burden fell on Shen Xiangqiang.

The second picture shows Shen Xiangqiang and other 4 family members, together with 5 vehicles in front of the newly-built house in May, 2017. Shen Xiangqiang contracted an apple orchard, a peach orchard and 6,670 square meters of land. He does the farm work at home in busy seasons and finds temporary jobs in cities in slack season, securing an annual income exceeding 40,000 yuan.

The remote mountainous Niuzhai Village enjoys a sound ecological environment and bounteous natural resources. Relying on the rich natural endowment, Niuzhai Village has developed ecological tourism, built an example of rural revitalization, and energized local agriculture, improving rural income and ensuring a happy life. Shen Xiangqiang is just an example of those benefiting from this transition.

Photo by Zhang Jian

助学贷款圆了大学梦

2017 年，临沂市沂南县生源地信用助学贷款受理现场，顺利办理好助学贷款后，父女俩开心地笑了。

为了帮助困难家庭的学生顺利完成学业，山东省从 2008 年正式启动生源地信用助学贷款。多年来，根据实际需要，山东省不断调整生源地信用助学贷款政策，切实解决了寒门学子求学的经济难题，为他们的成才之路扫除了障碍。目前，山东已经建立起从学前教育到研究生教育各学段全覆盖的资助政策体系，不让学生因家庭经济困难而辍学。

杜昱葆 摄

Student loan enables her to go to college

A father and his daughter from Yinan County of Linyi City are laughing after procedures to apply for student loan have been completed.

To help students from impoverished families to continue with their education, Shandong officially launched the program allowing students to apply for loan in their hometown in 2008. Over the years, Shandong has been improving this program in line with students' needs, which has solved the financial problems of students from poor families and helped to remove barriers lying in their way to receive higher education. Up to now, Shandong has established a sound policy support system covering various stages of education from pre-primary education to postgraduate education, avoiding dropping out due to financial difficulties.

Photo by Du Yubao

小辣椒红遍万里古丝路

青岛胶州在新疆独创辣椒扶贫模式。

通过辣椒小产业优势互补，助推扶贫大协作共赢发展，实现了东西互助手拉手，共同致富奔小康的目标。

胶州将辣椒发展成为特色产业扶贫，有着得天独厚的优势。胶州是目前全国最大的辣椒加工出口集散地，同时拥有辣椒新品种研发培育的基础。而新疆地区光热资源充足，无霜期长，昼夜温差大，利用通畅的铁路，胶州和乌鲁木齐之间可以实现便捷的物流运输。诸多优势促成了胶州将辣椒产业作为援疆的重要方式。

一颗颗红辣椒不仅让当地老百姓走上致富路，也串起了深厚的民族情。

Jiaozhou, China's exporter of chili

Jiaozhou, a county-level city of Qingdao, has developed a new model of poverty reduction through chili farming in Xinjiang.

This new model has brought together respective strengths of both regions in this industry in collaboration between the east and the west. It boosts poverty reduction and win-win development, and helps to achieve the goal of common prosperity and a well-off life.

Jiaozhou City enjoys unique natural endowment to develop the model of poverty reduction through chili growing. Jiaozhou is the largest hub in China for the processing and export of chilies, with the capability in the R&D and cultivation of new species of chilies. Meanwhile, Xinjiang boasts abundant sunshine and heat resources, a long frost-free season and big temperature difference between day and night. The railway services also enable the convenient logistics between Jiaozhou and Urumqi. Many favorable conditions have made chili growing an important way to provide assistance to Xinjiang by Jiaozhou.

Chili growing has not only created a better life for residents in Xinjiang, but also fostered a close bond among different ethnic groups.

VR 进课堂

2017 年 10 月，青岛市崂山区晓望小学 VR 教室，孩子们正在进行沉浸式体验。

随着 VR 技术的迅猛发展，"VR+ 教育"加快了教育信息化的步伐。VR 教室里，整个教学过程的沉浸感和互动性得到增强，学生可以更好地感受到学习的乐趣，真正实现能对话的课堂。

VR in classroom

In October, 2017, students in Xiaowang Primary School in Laoshan District of Qingdao City experience VR technology in an immersive way.

With the rapid development of VR technology, the "VR plus education" mode has accelerated the application of IT in the education sector. The VR technology has made the teaching process more immersive and interactive, allowing students to better understand the fun in study and interact with the learning materials.

银杏树下的美好时光

2017 年 11 月 8 日，山东省郯城县重坊镇徐出口村，一位母亲带着俩娃快乐出行。

王剑 摄

Mother and her two children

On November 8, 2017, a mother walks happily with her two children in Xuchukou Village, Chongfang Town, Tancheng County of Shandong.

Photo by Wang Jian

（上页图说）

朝霞与天鹅齐飞

每年 10 月，天鹅成群结队飞抵荣成。

朝阳喷薄而出，朝霞为湖面涂上一层迷人的橘黄色，天鹅迎着红日飞翔，或是在苍苍芦苇中追逐嬉戏，或悠闲自在地漫步……这些高雅的生灵宛若天外来客。这是在荣成天鹅湖常见的万物和谐共生的景象，亦是美不胜收的画卷。

2012 年以来，荣成市加大对天鹅湖生态的保护力度，采取多种措施提高湿地生态质量，清淤、整治堤坝，实施湿地修复工程，改造升级污水处理系统等，取得了显著成效。

马世民 摄

Swans flying at dawn

Groups of swans fly to Rongcheng City every October.

At rosy dawn when the sun rises above the sea level and the morning glow paints the lake with charming saffron, swans, like elegant creatures from another planet, would fly against the red sun, play in reed bushes or just walk about. This is a common scene of harmonious coexistence of every species in the Swan Lake of Rongcheng. It presents a picture whose beauty is beyond description.

Since 2012, Rongcheng has stepped up preservation of the ecological system in the Swan Lake through measures to improve wetland ecology, such as dredging riverbeds, consolidating banks, restoring wetland, and transforming and upgrading the sewage system, with obvious results achieved.

Photo by Ma Shimin

俺们的快乐生活

2017 年，在全国"阳光家园"示范机构——微山县残疾人托养中心。

残疾人托养服务，是帮助智力、精神和重度肢体残疾人克服社会认知和参与能力以及自理能力方面的障碍，平等参与社会生活，减轻残疾人家庭负担，促进社会和谐的有效手段。

2016—2019 年，山东省共投入 4 亿多元为近 10 万名贫困残疾人提供了居家托养、日间照料、寄宿托养照料等服务，解放了 3 万余户家庭的有效劳动力，减轻了贫困残疾人家庭的负担。

Happy life for people with disabilities

This picture is taken in 2017 in a national demonstration institution of Sunshine Home—Care Center for Disabled People in Weishan County.

For people who suffer from intellectual, mental and serious physical disabilities and have troubles in taking care of themselves, nursery service is effective in promoting equal social involvement, easing the burden on their families and promoting social harmony.

From 2016 to 2019, Shandong spent over 400 million yuan providing in-home care, daily care, and boarding care services for nearly 100 thousand people with disabilities, offering job opportunities to more than 30 thousand households and easing the burden over families with disabled members.

跑起来，生命更精彩

2017 年，泰山国际登山节开跑。

依托泰山得天独厚的旅游优势，泰安市自 1987 年开始举办登山节，至今已举办了 30 多年。泰山国际登山节已经成为泰安市一张靓丽的城市名片，规模和影响日益扩大，有利于促进旅游和体育产业深度融合，对繁荣赛事经济，起到了积极的推动作用。

Race to the top of Mount Tai

Climbers dash out in the International Mount Tai Climbing Festival in 2017.

Endowed with rich tourism resources, Tai'an City has held more than 30 sessions of International Mount Tai Climbing Festival since 1987. The festival is a shining brand name of the city. With growing scale and influence, it is now an impetus for sport and tourism integration and wider economic impact.

今天是俺的生日

2017 年 11 月 18 日，邹平县长山镇东尉村老年公寓内，大家正在为老人过生日。

老有所养、老有所乐，不仅是子女的义务，也是全社会的责任。面对滚滚而来的"银发浪潮"，东尉村不断完善养老保障体系，调动积极因素，让每一个老年人都能安享晚年，让尊老、爱老、敬老、养老成为最美丽的风景。

Today is my birthday

Grandpa is celebrating his birthday with friends at a senior apartment in Dongwei Village, Changshan Town, Zouping County on November 18, 2017.

Care and happiness for the elderly is not only the obligation of their children, but also the responsibility of the society. Faced with a growing number of the aged, Dongwei Village improves its elderly care system, and keeps everyone motivated to make sure that the elderly are respected and cared for.

不破不立

2018 年 3 月 7 日晚，张瑞敏在哈佛商学院进行公开演讲，吸引了哈佛大学、麻省理工学院、波士顿大学等顶尖大学学生的参与。

改革开放之初，齐鲁大地春风浩荡。海尔集团就是在这样的时代背景下创立于青岛，不过当时，它是一家濒临倒闭的集体小厂。1985 年，张瑞敏接到用户的来信，说冰箱存在问题，他带人检查仓库，发现 400 多台冰箱中竟然有 76 台不合格。当时一台冰箱的价格顶一个工人三年多的工资，而且供不应求，有人建议，将这些不合格的冰箱便宜卖给员工。但张瑞敏决定，让生产冰箱的职工亲手把不合格的冰箱全部砸掉。这一砸，砸掉的是旧模式，砸出的是企业管理的新体系。一直以来，以海尔为首的山东企业，以卓尔不凡的创举，激发企业活力，争当引领改革创新的典范。

A case study on business success given at Harvard

Zhang Ruimin, CEO of Haier Group, gives a lecture at Harvard Business School in Boston on March 7, 2018. Top students at Harvard, MIT, and Boston University come to the lecture.

Haier Group was founded in Qingdao City when China's reform and opening-up started to gain momentum, although it was only a small refrigerator factory at that time which seemed unlikely to survive. In 1985, a complaint letter was sent to Zhang Ruimin, saying there were quality problems with their refrigerators. He checked the warehouses, and found 76 substandard refrigerators out of 400. In those years, one refrigerator cost 3 years' salaries of a factory worker, and still fell short of demand. Some suggested selling the defective ones to their own staff at a lower price. Zhang Ruimin refused and decided to ask their workers to smash all 76 refrigerators. Gone with the smash was the old style. Instead, a new management system was put in place. Since then, Shandong businesses, with Haier among the top ones, have been striving all along to be the fine example of innovation, invigoration and excellence.

风雨兼程

2018 年 4 月 13 日雨夜，外卖小哥卢法可取餐后，准备给客户送餐。

每逢节假日，仍有千千万万劳动者坚守工作岗位，其中有个群体尤为引人注目。大街小巷都是他们奔波的身影，这就是"外卖小哥"。他们奔走在大街小巷，风雨无阻，兢兢业业。

工作虽然很辛苦，但他们都心怀美好梦想，卢法可希望能在老家县城买套房子，让妻子和儿子过上更好的日子。

杨超 摄

Deliver food orders in rain

On a rainy night on April 13, 2018, Lu Fake, a deliveryman, gets the food and is about to hit the road.

Hundreds of thousands of people, including deliverymen, stay on their posts during holidays. They rush at every corner of the city, come rain or shine.

Though work is tough, they all aspire to a better life. Lu Fake hopes to buy an apartment in his hometown, and provides a better life for his wife and son.

Photo by Yang Chao

阅读的美好时光

2018 年 4 月，在寿光市三元朱村农家书屋里，村民正在享受快乐的阅读时光。

自 2007 年农家书屋建设全面开展以来，山东省在全国率先实现农家书屋行政村全覆盖。目前，山东省先后建成农家书屋近 8 万个，建成数量居全国首位。

遍布乡村的农家书屋通过开展技能培训、组织阅读等活动，用精神食粮丰富村民的业余生活，为农村精神文明建设增强内力，让广大农民群众共享社会文明发展的成果。

杨超 摄

A rural library

Villagers are enjoying their reading time in the rural library in Sanyuanzhu Village, Shouguang City in April 2018.

Shandong started to build rural libraries in 2007, and it was the first province in China that saw every village with one library. Nearly 80,000 rural libraries have been built, topping the national list in number.

By organizing reading activities and skills training, rural libraries help enrich people's lives, advance cultural and ethical progress, and allow everyone in rural areas to benefit from social development.

Photo by Yang Chao

在晨光熹微中出发

2018 年 5 月，两位骑友正在东营孤岛槐林风景区内快乐骑行。

一辆单车，一个背包，路就在脚下，大自然就在身边。阳光洒在身上，万虑顿息。

Morning ride

Two riders are cycling happily in the woods of Huailin scenic area, Gudao Town, Dongying City in May 2018.

With a bicycle and a bag, road lying ahead, and nature around, all worries clear off in that dawn light.

梦想的旋律

2018 年 6 月，落日余晖下，青岛市民在小鱼山公园练习小提琴。

以开放之势，领风气之先。2018 年，对青岛来说，是砥砺奋进的一年，是承载希望的一年，更是实现梦想的一年。

国际 VR 影像周、管乐艺术周、国际陶瓷艺术展、国际书法双年展、青岛婚恋文化周、青岛赏花会、世界大学生时尚设计大赛……文化活动精彩纷呈；组建最强招商团队，"双招双引"工作如火如荼；打造国际一流营商环境，"一次办好""一窗通办""5 分钟政务服务圈"将政务服务改革落到实处；"助老食堂""喘息式"养老服务，完善养老服务，人民生活更加舒心。

这悠扬的琴声，悦耳动听的旋律，就是老百姓幸福生活的最佳体现。

董志刚 摄

Morning melody

A young lady is playing the violin at dusk in Xiaoyushan Park, Qingdao City in June 2018.

2018 was a year of dreams coming true for Qingdao and its citizens.

For culture lovers, there was international VR week, wind music week, international ceramic art exhibition, calligraphy exhibition, cultural week of romance, flower festival, world university student fashion design competition, etc. For investment and talent, highly competitive teams for attracting investment and high-caliber talents were formed. For businesses, the best team stood ready to build world-class business environment with one-stop services, process integration, and 5-minute circle of governmental services. For senior citizens, special supporting canteens and short-term elderly care were put in place.

The melodious music best reflected people's happy life.

Photo by Dong Zhigang

脊梁

2018 年 6 月 6 日，泰山挑山工正在埋头负重攀登。

当你游览泰山，在陡峭的十八盘拾级而上，两腿如灌重铅的时候，你身旁会有这样一群人默默走过，他们挑一百多斤的担子，肩负重荷，步履艰难地前行——这些人就是泰山挑山工。泰山挑山工，一根扁担，双肩挑，挑出泰山无限风景，挑出撼动人心的精神力量。

姜东涛 摄

Carry supplies to top of Mount Tai

A heaver carrying supplies is climbing up the stairs of Mount Tai on June 6, 2018.

When you are traveling on Mount Tai, and ascending step by step on the steep stairs of Shibapan (the eighteen bends, the most adventurous part of stairs on Mount Tai), feeling your legs overburdened, you might notice some people trudging up the mountain with heavy loads weighing over 50 kilos. They are the heavers on Mount Tai. With one carrying pole, they illustrate the fabulous scenery and the inspiring power of perseverance.

Photo by Jiang Dongtao

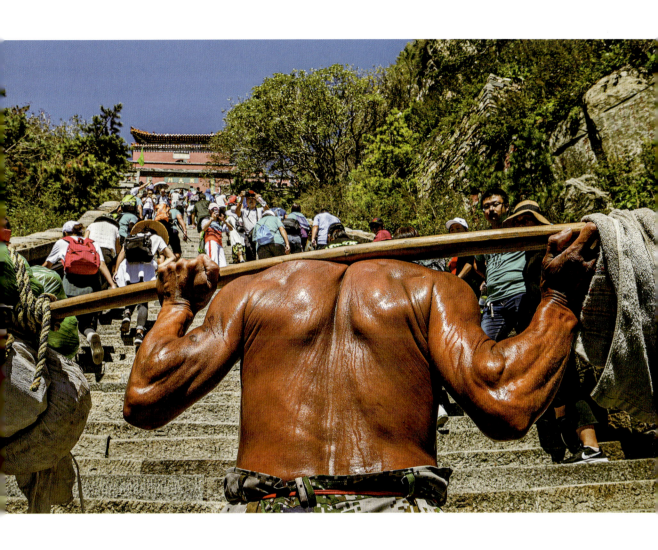

医者仁心

2018年8月，临沂市沂水县院东头镇乡村医生张在吉在给孙子孙女讲解针灸穴位。张在吉的父亲也是乡村医生，张家世代行医，传到儿子张德庆这一代已是第三代。

周围几个村子里的年轻人大多在外谋生，留守在家的大都是老人和孩子。村民们有个头疼脑热的都会来找张德庆，他对待每一名病人都十分认真。他时刻牢记着祖父和父亲的教导："做医生，不能糊弄人。"

饶琦 摄

This is how acupuncture works

Zhang Zaiji, a rural doctor in Yuandongtou Town, Yishui County, Linyi City, is explaining acupuncture points to his grandchildren in August 2018.

Zhang Zaiji's father was also a rural doctor, so is his son Zhang Deqing.

Most young people in the neighboring villages work away from home, leaving the elderly and the children in the hometown, who turn to Zhang Deqing whenever feeling ill. Zhang Deqing treats every patient seriously, because he always bears the family motto in mind, "A doctor never skimps on his job."

Photo by Rao Qi

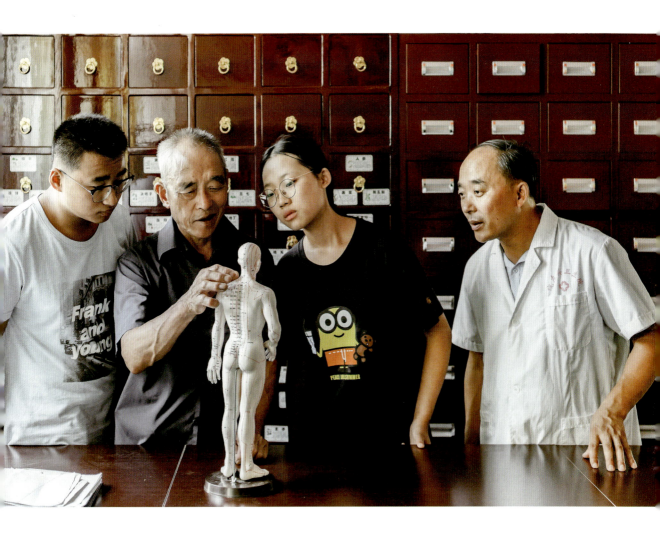

"照亮"致富路

2018 年 8 月，马崮峪光伏发电扶贫项目初具规模。

马崮峪光伏发电项目是沂水县投资额最高、单体规模最大、受益覆盖面最广的光伏扶贫项目。

光伏发电清洁环保，技术可靠，收益稳定，既适合建设户用和村级小电站，也适合建设较大规模的集中式电站，还可以结合农业、林业等开展多种"光伏＋"应用项目。

光伏发电，用太阳能"照亮"致富路。

李春余 摄

A solar power project in rural area

The photovoltaic poverty alleviation project in Maguyu Village begins to take shape in August 2018.

This project is the largest one of its kind in Yishui County in terms of investment, single project scale, and coverage.

Photovoltaic power generation is environmentally friendly with proven technology and stable returns, suitable for small power stations at household and village levels, big centralized power stations and also other application scenarios, such as in agriculture and forestry where the "Photovoltaic Plus" model can be applied.

It is photovoltaic that lights up the road to prosperity with solar power.

Photo by Li Chunyu

历史的选择

2018 年 8 月，威海刘公岛"历史选择展馆"中充满张力的雕塑。

历史上，在刘公岛海域发生的中日"甲午海战"，把刘公岛深深刻进每一个中国人的记忆中。

今天的刘公岛碧海蓝天，草木茂盛，来自全国各地的游客纷至沓来，走进"历史选择展馆"，探寻中华民族伟大复兴的历史密码。

张平 摄

Never forget aggression against China

A big sculpture in the Choice of History Exhibition Hall on Liugong Island in Weihai City in August 2018

Liugong Island is remembered by every Chinese for the Sino-Japanese War of 1894-1895 which took place in its offshore areas.

Today's Liugong Island, with blue sea, azure sky, and lush vegetation, attracts travelers from all parts of the country. Many of them come here and visit the exhibition hall to decode China's journey to its national rejuvenation.

Photo by Zhang Ping

"德不孤，必有邻"

2018年9月，青岛市"邻居节"，李沧区上流佳苑社区活动现场。

2004年，青岛市原四方区回应市民建议，在海伦路街道试点举办首届社区"邻居节"。2013年，原市北区、四方区合并设立新的市北区，"邻居节"活动在全区所有街道社区全面展开。2016年起，青岛市在全市10个区市推广开展"邻居节"活动，每年一届，由各区市轮流主办，努力打造全市精神文明建设新生活、新亮点。现在，"邻居节"已经是青岛人一年一次的约定。

从一个居民的建议衍生到全市的百花齐放，"邻居节"在青岛生根发芽、不断普及，已经成为展示青岛市公民道德建设和思想政治工作成果的亮点品牌。

Lively community activities

This is a glimpse of Qingdao Neighbor's Day at Shangliu Jiayuan Community, Licang District in September 2018.

In 2004, in response to citizen's advice, the former Sifang District of Qingdao started its pilot program of Neighbor's Day in Hailun Road Sub-district. In 2013, the Neighbor's Day was extended to the whole newly-incorporated Shibei District (an integration of the former Shibei District and Sifang District), and then to all the 10 districts of the city in 2016. It has become an annual festival held by different districts in turn from then on.

Starting from one single piece of advice to a festival celebrated by the whole city, Neighbor's Day has grown into a brand project demonstrating the governance and cultural development of Qingdao.

美丽乡村，我们来了

2018 年 9 月，来自清华大学的志愿者与乡村振兴服务队的工作人员在莒南，共建社会主义新农村。

2018 年，山东省组织开展"千名干部下基层"工作，从省直部门（单位）选派 1000 名干部，组成 50 支乡村振兴服务队和 50 支高质量发展服务队，深入基层，摸实情、出实招、办实事，成为村民的"贴心人"和乡村发展的"引路人"。

Volunteers assist rural development

Volunteers from Tsinghua University and members of rural vitalization team in Ju'nan County join hands to promote rural development in September 2018.

In 2018, Shandong selected and dispatched 1,000 officials from provincial departments to primary-level institutions. They formed 50 working teams supporting rural revitalization and another 50 focusing on the high-quality development. They have been dedicated to spotting problems, offering solutions and taking practical actions as close friends of villagers and facilitators for rural development.

凝望

2018 年 9 月，新时代"沂蒙扶贫六姐妹"到"沂蒙六姐妹"纪念馆学习。

革命战争年代，沂蒙地区无数儿女奔赴前线，后方的妇女们也主动挑起拥军的重担，其中以张玉梅、伊廷珍、杨桂英、伊淑英、冀贞兰、公方莲"沂蒙六姐妹"为代表，她们不分昼夜烙煎饼，为保障前线供给做出了不可磨灭的贡献。在新时代脱贫攻坚的路上，沂蒙革命老区又涌现出新的"沂蒙六姐妹"，她们靠坚强的意志，带领群众脱贫致富，为革命老区的扶贫攻坚贡献力量，她们被誉为新时代"沂蒙扶贫六姐妹"。

尹召功 摄

Pay tribute to six women who assisted war efforts

The six women devoted to poverty alleviation in Yimeng in modern times visit the memorial for the six women who assisted war efforts in September 2018.

During the War of Liberation, women at home away from the battlefield took up the burden to support the front line. The six women, namely Zhang Yumei, Yi Tingzhen, Yang Guiying, Yi Shuying, Ji Zhenlan, Gong Fanglian, were the fine examples of them. They made Chinese pancakes day and night, making indelible contribution to securing the front-line supplies. In the tough battle against poverty in the new era, another six women come forth, and dedicate themselves to the poverty eradication efforts in the old revolutionary base areas.

Photo by Yin Zhaogong

心中的牡丹

　　菏泽市巨野县是全国唯一的"中国农民绘画之乡"，也是"中国工笔画之乡"。工笔牡丹画是菏泽巨野的当家画种，它在继承中国传统工笔技法的基础上，结合现代工艺手段，工整典雅，色彩绚丽，展示了牡丹的富贵吉祥，寓意新时代繁花似锦、国富民强。

　　近年来，随着国家对传统文化的重视和支持，凭借书画艺术和书画产业特有的潜力和活力，依托优越的地理条件和优厚的扶持政策，巨野县书画产业迅速发展。

　　目前，全县已建成了30多个书画院和培训点，带动形成了50多个绘画专业村，1000多个专业户。从事创作、销售、装裱等书画产业的人员有15000余人，可谓"家家溢墨香，户户绘新枝"。

Painting peony for orders placed

Juye County of Heze City, the only county in China known as home of farmer's painting, is also a hot land of Gongbi painting, a traditional Chinese painting using highly detailed brushstrokes that delimits details precisely. Gongbi Peonies is the main type of painting in Juye County. Integrating traditional and modern techniques, it features elaborate, elegant and high-colored blooming peonies, symbolizing prosperity of the nation and the people in the new era.

In recent years, with growing attention to and support for traditional culture and thanks to the unique potential and vitality of calligraphy and painting and the art industry, favorable geographical conditions, and enabling supporting policies, the calligraphy and painting industry in Juye has boomed.

Now in Juye, there are more than 30 calligraphy and painting schools and training institutions, with more than 50 villages and over 1,000 households specialized in painting, and over 15,000 people either painting, mounting, framing or selling the paintings.

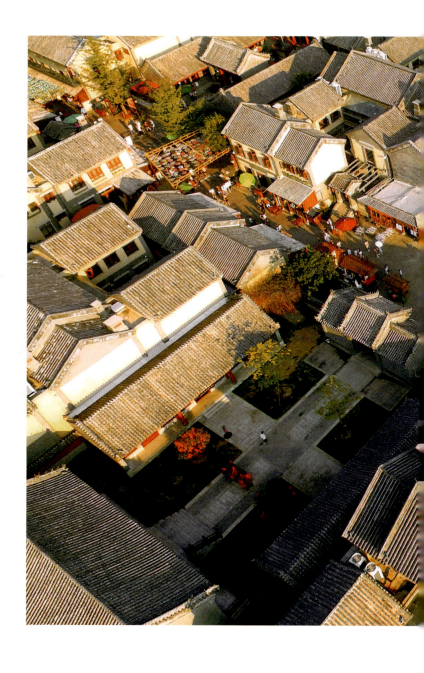

乡村小镇，乡土生"金"

2018 年 7 月 21 日，游客在郯城县马头镇南园街观光游览。

郯城县马头镇南园街充分发挥区域集市大和特色小吃多的优势，倾力打造"小吃一条街"和"小吃文化节"两张名片。目前已建成仿古街、小吃街、百花园、戏楼等商贸、文化设施，成功举办了两届"小吃文化节"，开展了丰富多彩的"非遗"展演、书画展览等活动，实现了"文化搭台、经贸唱戏"的助农增收目标。

房德华 摄

A tourist street in a village

Travelers are touring around at Nanyuan Street, Matou Town, Tancheng County, on July 21, 2018.

Nanyuan Street gives full play to its advantages of big county fair and numerous local snacks, and creates two brand names out of it, namely the Street of Snacks and the Snacks Cultural Festival. Antique streets, snack streets, gardens, and traditional theaters have been built. Two Snacks Cultural Festivals were held, putting on exhibitions and performances of intangible cultural heritages, calligraphy and painting, and increasing the local farmers' income with new business opportunities.

Photo by Fang Dehua

奔跑吧，少年

2018 年 10 月，济南历下区实验小学的孩子们。

曹清雅　摄

After class

The photo shows students of Jinan Lixia Experimental Primary School in October, 2018.

Photo by Cao Qingya

海的女儿

2018 年 10 月，世界大学生时尚设计大赛在青岛栈桥开秀。

伴随着洒向海面的第一缕阳光，青岛栈桥化身"巨型 T 台"，上演了一场时尚走秀。历经百年的青岛栈桥，首次作为秀场和大片实景拍摄场地，也是国内首次将标志性景点对学生设计师开放。一组组国际感十足，洋溢着青春创意的时尚作品，与栈桥进行了一次跨越百年的对话。

青岛以开放的姿态，呈现出全球不同国家、民族和文化的设计语言与时尚态度，融汇出熠熠生辉的时尚名片。

董志刚 摄

Fashion show by the sea in Qingdao

The International Students Fashion Design Gala is put on in the dawn light on Qingdao Zhanqiao Pier in October 2018.

It was the first time for Zhanqiao Pier, as a century-old architecture, to be the site for a fashion show and its shooting, and it was also the first time for a symbolic scenic spot in China to open to student designers. This was a dialog between the historical pier and the innovative fashion designs brimming with international and youthful elements.

The International Students Fashion Design Gala has become a fashion brand of Qingdao, who opens up its arms and showcases the designs and fashion of different nations, ethnic groups and cultures of the world.

Photo by Dong Zhigang

雏凤清于老凤声

2019 年 6 月，济南皮影戏传承人李娟在表演皮影戏。

相比于其他表演艺术，皮影戏对表演者的要求更高，它不仅考验表演者嘴上说、念、打、唱的功夫，而且需要表演者手上活灵活现地演绎各种角色，脚下还要敲击锣鼓进行乐器伴奏。"一口叙说千古事，双手对舞百万兵"，济南皮影布景上的这副对联形象地阐释了皮影戏的独特韵味。作为济南皮影戏传承人的李娟，让人看到皮影戏这种古老艺术形式的创新和活力。

近年来，由于国家对传统文化的重视，李娟作为济南皮影戏的传承人，受邀到过二十多个国家演出。为了满足外国朋友的需要，她还创作了英语剧。

为将皮影艺术发扬光大，李娟不仅组织济南皮影研学游，还在百花洲设立传统工艺工作站，每个周末都有很多大人和孩子来学习，成为大家观看学习济南皮影戏的聚集地。

杨超 摄

How to give a shadow show

Li Juan, an inheritor of Jinan shadow puppetry, is performing in June 2019.

Shadow puppetry is more demanding for performers than other art forms. Artists need to master special techniques such as singing, falsetto, simultaneous manipulation of several puppets using two hands, and the ability to play various musical instruments with feet. As a couplet on the backdrop of the play goes, shadow puppetry is an art that has "a mouth as the narrator of stories through ages, two hands as commander of troops". Li Juan shows the innovation and the vitality of this ancient art.

In recent years, China has attached great importance to traditional culture. Li Juan, as an inheritor of Jinan shadow puppetry, has been invited to perform in more than 20 countries. She even creates English plays to share the art with foreign friends.

To take the art even further, Li Juan has organized study tours in Jinan, and set up a studio on traditional craftsmanship in Baihua Pond cultural block, attracting a lot of people including children to enjoy and learn about shadow puppetry every weekend.

Photo by Yang Chao

俺家

2019 年 6 月，章丘三涧溪党总支书记高淑贞真抓实干、奋发有为，让一个贫困村发展成为"全国乡村治理示范村"。

无论是脱贫攻坚还是乡村振兴，都离不开"领头雁"担当作为。"头雁"领飞，乡村振兴必能展翅翱翔。

三涧溪村脱贫致富，村集体净资产上亿元，人均年收入 2.8 万元，荣膺"全国民主法治示范村""全国平安家庭创建先进单位""全国妇联基层组织建设示范村"等殊荣。2019 年底，又被评为"全国乡村治理示范村"。

涧溪春晓，风光正好。

A poor rural village transformed

Gao Shuzhen, the Party Secretary of the Sanjianxi Village Committee, Zhangqiu District, has dedicated herself to the development of the village, and succeeded in turning the poor village into a National Demonstration Village on Rural Governance in June 2019.

Neither poverty alleviation nor rural vitalization would succeed without a leader who shoulders due responsibility and works down to earth. This leader is the key to revitalizing rural areas.

Now Sanjianxi Village has shaken off poverty and been much better-off with the net collective assets exceeding 100 million yuan, and an annual per capita income of 28,000 yuan. It has also won several national awards on democracy and rule of law, happy family and development of primary-level women's federation. In 2019, it was recognized as a National Demonstration Village on Rural Governance.

Like its trees in spring, Sanjianxi Village is thriving.

小小少年

2019 年 9 月，济宁市金乡县，正在进行体育运动的阳光少年。

校园里的体育课程、升学考试中的体育测试……在教育体系中，体育正越来越受重视。从家长到学校，正逐渐形成一种共识：体育是教育不可或缺的一环。

金乡，这个位于四省交界处的鲁西南小城，是李白笔下"青山横北郭，白水绕东城"的诗意所在，也是人们印象中的"大蒜之乡"。近年来，金乡县教育建设模式引发广泛关注，教育事业持续迸发新动能，一跃成为鲁西南地区"现象级"教育高地。

在金乡，校园京剧、地方戏曲、书法、陶艺、体育等教育已产生了品牌效应，丰富多彩的活动次第展开、别开生面。

郭尧 摄

Young football players

A group of boys are playing football in Jinxiang County, Jining City in September 2019.

In the education system, physical education is drawing greater attention, as evidenced by the PE courses in the curriculum and PE tests in the admission examinations. A consensus is gradually taking shape between parents and schools, namely, sport is an indispensable part of education.

Jinxiang, the "hometown of garlic", is a small county in southwestern Shandong at the junction of four provinces. It is a poetic place just like the poet Li Bai once said, "The lush mountains lie on the north side of the city, and the sparkling water surrounds the east side." In recent years, the education model of Jinxiang County has received wide attention. Brimming with new momentum in its education sector, Jinxiang has become a pacesetter in educational development in southwestern Shandong.

In Jinxiang, educational activities such as Peking opera, local opera, calligraphy, pottery, and physical education have formed brand effects, and a variety of activities are being launched one after another.

Photo by Guo Yao

"第一"

2019 年 9 月，广饶县大王镇延集村，人们在参观山东农村第一个党支部纪念馆。1925 年，这里诞生了山东省农村第一个党支部。

中共延集支部是山东省最早的农村党支部，在山东省农村党的建设历史上有着极其重要的地位和作用。1923 年春，延伯真经王尽美、邓恩铭介绍加入中国共产党，成为山东省早期共产党员之一。1924 年 8 月，延伯真回到家乡延集村开展工作，他先在本村介绍知识青年延安吉入党，又到寿光县张家庄介绍张玉山、王云山二人入党，并帮助建立了中共寿（光）广（饶）小组，张玉山任组长，延安吉、王云山分别任委员。

1925 年 2 月，两县分别建立党支部。中共延集支部建立后，延安吉任书记，隶属于中共济南地方执行委员会，是东营地区的第一个党支部。

延集党支部建立后，先后发展延俊章等十几人入党，使党的力量不断壮大。同时还开展了销售《向导》周报、《新青年》、《中国青年》等进步刊物的工作，销售刊物所得的钱，全部交给上级党组织。为争取和团结农民群众，他们连续创办农民夜校，教农民识字，参加群众最多时有 300 人左右。

杨超 摄

The first branch of the Party set up in rural Shandong in 1925

People visit the memorial hall of the first Party branch in rural Shandong in Yanji Village, Dawang Town, Guangrao County in September 2019.

In 1925, the Yanji Branch of the Communist Party of China, the first Party branch in rural Shandong was established here. It played a crucial role in the history of Party building in rural areas of the province. In the spring of 1923, Yan Bozhen joined the CPC through the introduction of Wang Jinmei and Deng Enming, two founders of the CPC, becoming one of the first CPC members in Shandong Province. In August 1924, Yan Bozhen returned to his hometown of Yanji Village. From there, he introduced Yan Anji to join the Party. Then he introduced Zhang Yushan and Wang Yunshan to the Party in Zhangjiazhuang Village, Shouguang County. Yan Bozhen also helped establish the CPC Shouguang-Guangrao Group, with Zhang Yushan as the group leader, and Yan Anji and Wang Yunshan as group committee members.

In February 1925, Party branches were formed in those two counties respectively. The CPC Yanji Branch, in which Yan Anji served as the Secretary, was affiliated to the CPC Jinan Regional Executive Committee, and was the first Party branch in Dongying.

After the establishment of the CPC Yanji Branch, the Party grew stronger by admitting more than a dozen people including Yan Junzhang to the branch. They began to sell progressive publications such as *Guide Weekly*, *New Youth* and *China Youth* and submitted all the money to the Party organization at higher level. In order to unite more people from rural areas, they established night schools to teach farmers to read, helping as many as 300 people at one point.

Photo by Yang Chao

"蔬菜硅谷"

2019 年 9 月，寿光全国蔬菜质量标准中心的基因编辑育种实验室。

改革开放初期，这里诞生了冬暖式大棚，结束了中国北方冬季吃不上新鲜蔬菜的历史。大棚技术逐渐传播至全国 20 多个省区，一场改写农业历史的"绿色革命"在寿光掀起。时光荏苒，科技创新在这里再次掀起了产业升级的高潮，无土栽培、智慧大棚、分子育种……寿光正在乡村振兴的道路上探索前行。

以科技创新为驱动力，寿光大棚的产业发展摆脱了片面追求产量的野蛮生长之路，走出了一条"量""质"并重的双轮驱动的绿色发展之路。

打造中国"蔬菜硅谷"是寿光的目标，也是持续不竭的发展动力。目前，中国智慧农业装备示范园区、现代农业高新技术集成示范区、蔬菜产业创新研发基地三大高科技园区作为中国"蔬菜硅谷"的核心区已现雏形。

李炳泉 摄

A gene laboratory for growing vegetables

The photo shows the Laboratory for Genome Editing and Breeding at the National Vegetable Quality Standard Center in Shouguang in September 2019.

At the beginning of the reform and opening-up, winter greenhouses were established in Shouguang, ending the history of not having fresh vegetables in northern China in winter. Greenhouse technologies gradually spread to more than 20 provinces and regions across the country, setting off from Shouguang a "green revolution" that rewrote the history of agriculture. Time flies. Technological innovation, such as soilless cultivation, smart greenhouse, and molecular breeding, has given rise to a new boom in industrial upgrading. Shouguang is blazing a new trail towards rural revitalization.

Driven by scientific and technological innovation, the greenhouse sector in Shouguang no longer focuses on quantity alone. Instead, it has embarked on a path of improving quality and quantity in parallel, making them the two wheels driving green development.

It is the goal and sustained driving force of Shouguang to build itself into China's "silicon valley of vegetables". At present, the core area of the valley is taking shape, composed of the National Demonstration Area for Smart Agricultural Equipment, Integrated Demonstration Area for Modern Agricultural High Technologies, and Innovation and R&D Base for Vegetable Industry.

Photo by Li Bingquan

第一船

2019 年 9 月 1 日，黄渤海结束为期 4 个月的休渔期，进入秋季开捕第一天。傍晚时分，山东青岛西海岸新区积米崖渔港码头，当天 12 时后出海作业的渔船陆续归来，带回久违的鱼虾蟹等海鲜，闻讯赶来的市民和游客早早等在码头，渔船一靠岸，就加入抢购的行列，品尝秋季第一船海鲜。

渔业经济迅猛发展背后是山东省在海洋生态保护方面的久久为功。2019 年，山东省生态环境厅印发实施《山东省海洋生态环境保护规划（2018—2020 年）》，决定将全省海域规划成 17 类 341 个分区进行管控，各分区实行不同的环境保护要求。

规划明确提出，要推进重点区域、重要生态系统从现有的分散分片保护转向集中成片的面上整体保护，实行海湾、海水、海岛、海滩、海岸的系统协调保护；加强海水养殖污染防控治理，加强船舶、港口污染防治管理，推进沿岸及海上垃圾污染防治；实施流域环境和近岸海域污染综合治理；加快构建海洋生态环境监测"一张网"。

朱春明 摄

First morning catch for the fishing season

At dusk of September 1, 2019, the first day of fishing in autumn after 4-month fishing off season in the Yellow Sea and Bohai Sea, fishing boats return fully loaded to Jimiya Fishing Wharf in Qingdao, and awaited citizens and tourists rush to buy the fresh seafood.

Behind the rapid development of the fishery economy is Shandong's unrelenting effort on marine environmental protection. In 2019, Shandong Provincial Department of Ecology and Environment issued and implemented the *Shandong Provincial Marine Environmental Protection Plan (2018—2020)*, in which the province's sea areas are divided into 17 categories and 341 districts, and each district follows different environmental protection requirements.

The plan clearly states that it is imperative to transform the current scattered and fragmented protection of key areas and important ecosystems to integrated protection, and implement coordinated protection of bays, seas, islands, beaches, and coasts. Steps should be taken to strengthen control of marine aquaculture pollution, improve the management of pollution prevention of ships and ports, and promote the treatment of coastal and offshore garbage pollution. Systemic measures should be carried out to control pollution in river basins and offshore areas, and establish a monitoring system for marine environment.

Photo by Zhu Chunming

一码在手，医保无忧

2019 年 11 月 24 日，全国医保电子凭证首发仪式在济南市举行。

医保电子凭证是医疗保障信息平台中参保人的唯一标识，是打通医保线上服务的金钥匙。与实体卡或其他电子卡相比，医保电子凭证有方便快捷、全国通用等突出优点。

参保人可以依此在全国办理有关医保业务，可以说"一码在手，医保无忧"。

山东作为开展医保电子凭证工作的先行试点省，对全面推进医保信息化建设，努力打造新时期医疗保障事业改革发展的"齐鲁样板"具有重要实践意义。

张宪政 摄

Medical insurance provided through QR code

A lady shows her QR code for medical insurance at the national launching ceremony of electronic certificate for medical insurance on November 24, 2019 in Jinan.

The electronic certificate for medical insurance is the only identification of the insured person on the medical insurance information platform, and is the golden key to access the online medical insurance services. Compared with physical cards or other electronic cards, the electronic certificate is more convenient and efficient, and can be used universally throughout the country.

Users can enjoy relevant medical insurance services across the country accordingly. It is fair to say that with the QR code in hand, there will be no worries in medical insurance.

Shandong, as a pilot province in rolling out electronic certificate for medical insurance, plays a significant role in facilitating IT application in medical insurance. It is now striving to build itself into a model of reforming and developing health care in the new era.

Photo by Zhang Xianzheng

奋斗的幸福　Happiness Earned Through Hard Work　187

蓝鲸 1 号

　　"蓝鲸"系列超深水钻井平台作为核心钻探装备，先后助力我国可燃冰首轮和第二轮试采成功。
　　由山东烟台中集来福士海洋工程有限公司建造的半潜式钻井平台——"蓝鲸 1 号"，是当今世界海洋钻井平台设计建造最高水平的代表。"蓝鲸 1 号"的横空出世，正是中集来福士走自主创新结出的硕果，作为大国重器，为中国制造贡献山东智慧和力量。

樊博 摄

A semi-submersible oil drilling rig

Blue Whale series of ultra-deep-water drilling rigs, as the core drilling equipment, have helped China's first and second rounds of extraction of combustible ice.

Blue Whale I, a semi-submersible drilling platform manufactured by Yantai CIMC Raffles Offshore Limited, is by far the most advanced semi-submersible drilling platform in the world. Blue Whale I is the fruit of the independent innovation of CIMC Raffles. Shandong, therefore, has contributed its wisdom and strength to "Made in China".

Photo by Fan Bo

"谢谢你，山东人"

来自山东的医护人员省下自己的水果送给患者吃，这名重症患者写下"谢谢你，山东人"。

2020年2月2日，一位湖北黄冈的新型冠状病毒感染的肺炎患者小兰在自己的微信朋友圈发了一条信息，感谢山东援助医疗队的精心照顾，还配了不少图片，引起众多网友关注，这就是其中一张。

小兰当时的病情比较重，家属来送过好几次水果，但需要转送好多次，不是很方便。怎样才能让小兰吃到水果成了医护队员的"心病"。医疗队的队员们每天都有水果餐，因此队员们便把水果攒了起来捎到医院。当李赞武和房晓杰进入病房值班时，便将水果送给小兰。小兰拿到后非常感动。

总有一种温暖，让我们泪流满面。致敬白衣天使!

A thank-you note from a Covid-19 patient in Hubei Province to doctors from Shandong

On February 2, 2020, Xiaolan, a patient with COVID-19 in Huanggang, Hubei Province writes down "Thank you, Shandong people" to two Shandong doctors, who have volunteered to come to Hubei for medical assistance and saved up their fruit for her.

On that day, Xiaolan posted a message and some pictures, including this one, on her WeChat Moments, thanking the Shandong medical aid team for their meticulous care, which attracted wide attention on the Internet.

Xiaolan was in a serious condition at the time, and her family had come to send her fruits several times, but it took several procedures before she could get them. Members of the Shandong medical team noticed this problem, and decided to save their daily shares of fruits and give them to the patient. That day when Doctor Li Zanwu and Fang Xiaojie were on duty, they gave the fruits to Xiaolan, and Xiaolan was deeply moved.

There is always a kind of warmth that moves us to tears. Tribute to the medical workers!

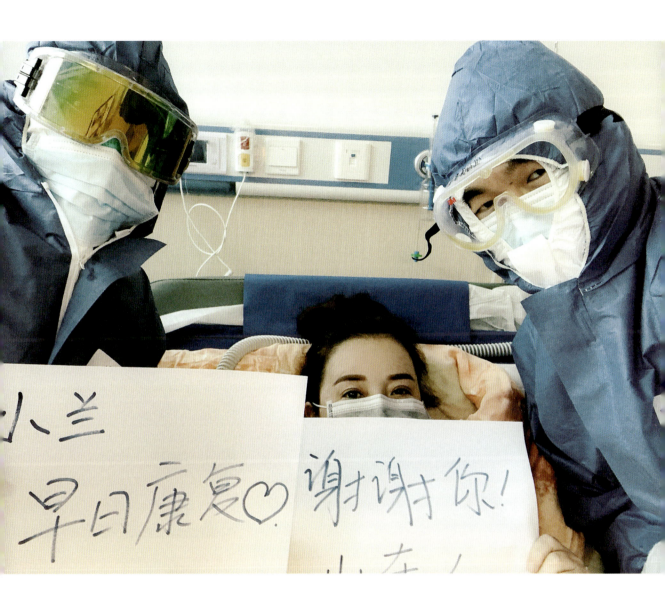

幸福的味道

2020 年 7 月 9 日，曲阜市石门山镇董庄北村贫困老人在幸福食堂开心用餐。

近年来，济宁市大力推进"幸福食堂"建设，贫困老人就餐免费，不仅有效解决了贫困老人吃饭难的问题，还为他们提供了一个精神交流的场所，提升了贫困老人的幸福感、获得感。

杨国庆 摄

Free meals for elder villagers

On July 9, 2020, poor elderly people of Dongzhuangbei Village, Shimenshan Town, Qufu City are dining happily in the Happiness Cafeteria.

In recent years, Jining City has been vigorously promoting the "Happiness Cafeteria", in which free meals are provided for the elderly poor. The cafeteria not only solves the problem of providing food for the elderly poor, but also serves as a place for them to communicate with others, thus enhancing their sense of fulfillment and happiness.

Photo by Yang Guoqing

泉子村的笑声

泉子村位于博山西南山区，村子位于海拔 800 米的山上，270 多户人家分散在山岭沟壑中，村里有 16 眼泉，是名副其实的泉子村。但前些年泉子村却是远近闻名的贫困村，十里八乡都知道"守着薄田，烧得柴草，住得石头房，有女不嫁泉子村"。

借助国家利好三农政策，2009 年，村里成立了农产品专业合作社，通过"合作社 + 基地 + 农户"的发展模式，带动村民就业。泉子村因地制宜，把闲置的农家院落整修装饰，打造成别致的乡间民宿。并让村民以土地入股的形式，把零散的土地整合起来，建起采摘园。经过多年发展，往昔冷清贫穷的小山村成为乡村旅游打卡地，全村共同致富奔小康。

苏昕 摄

Happy villagers

The picture shows the smiles of villagers from Quanzi Village.

Quanzi Village is located on a mountain 800 meters above sea level in the southwest mountainous area of Boshan District. More than 270 families are scattered in the mountains and ravines. There are 16 springs in the village, which makes the village live up to its name Quanzi (springs). However, Quanzi Village used to be known for its poverty. Its villagers farmed infertile land, burned firewood, lived in stone houses, and no women would like to marry a man from Quanzi Village.

Helped by China's favorable policies for agriculture, rural areas and farmers, the village established an agricultural product cooperative in 2009, which created job opportunities for villagers through the "cooperative + base + farmer households" model. According to local conditions, Quanzi Village renovated and decorated the idle farmyards and transformed them into countryside home stay hotels. With villagers becoming shareholders by pooling their lands, scattered lands were integrated into gardens for picking fruits and vegetables. After years of development, the once deserted and poor village has become a popular tourism spot, moving towards moderate prosperity.

Photo by Su Xin

小康之变

上图为 2015 年 10 月 11 日，淄博市高青县常家镇黄河滩区的五合庄村；下图为 2020 年 5 月 1 日，新建成的淄博市高青县常家镇常盛社区。

随着黄河滩区搬迁工作的推进，居民在当地政策支持下，挪了穷窝、断了穷根，努力奔小康。

高青县是淄博市唯一的沿黄县，位于常家镇的常盛社区是高青县第一个完成整建制搬迁的社区。常家镇的开河村、五合庄村 323 户 1050 名村民都搬到了这里。

为方便搬迁群众生产生活，高青县将滩区迁建工程与新型城镇化建设、美丽乡村建设相结合，外迁安置社区向县城或镇政府驻地集中。五合庄村村民迁入的常盛社区住宅楼采取"6+1"模式，一层为车库，便于群众存放农机具等设备，二至七层为带电梯住宅。常盛社区选址在高青县城规划区以内，紧邻经济开发区健康医药产业园，村民就业问题迎刃而解。社区东侧就是学校，周边医、养配套服务完善。

张维堂 摄

Photo above: A village transformed

The photo above shows the Wuhezhuang Village at the floodplain of the Yellow River of Changjia Town, Gaoqing County, Zibo City on October 11, 2015.

Photo below: A new resettlement village built

The photo below shows the newly built Changsheng Community in Changjia Town on May 1, 2020, where Wuhezhuang Village was relocated to.

With the advancement of the relocation of people living along the Yellow River, the residents, with the support of local policies, have moved away from the poor areas, and began to lead a more prosperous life.

Gaoqing County is the only county along the Yellow River in Zibo City. The Changsheng Community in Changjia Town is the first community in Gaoqing County to complete the relocation. 1,050 villagers from 323 households in Kaihe Village and Wuhezhuang Village of Changjia Town have moved here.

In order to facilitate the life and work of the relocated people, Gaoqing County combined the relocation project with new urbanization and beautiful countryside development, moving the relocated community near the county town or the town government. The residential buildings in Changsheng Community adopted the "6+1" model. The first floor is garages for storing agricultural machinery and other equipment, and the second to seventh floors are apartments with elevators. The Changsheng Community is close to the Health and Pharmaceutical Park of the Economic Development Zone, which provides enough jobs for villagers. The community is also equipped with schools to its east, and complete health care services and other amenities nearby.

Photo by Zhang Weitang

5G 助力智慧医疗

2020 年 9 月，青岛大学附属医院完成一例 5G 超远程泌尿外科手术。

当下科技领域最热、最受关注的莫过于人工智能、云计算、5G、物联网。人工智能在 5G 时代下，可提供更快的响应速度、更丰富的内容、更智能的应用模式以及更直观的用户体验。5G 不仅提升网速，而且将补齐制约人工智能发展的短板，成为驱动人工智能的新动力。

5G 助力智慧医疗，将实现快速急救、远程医疗、新健康管理、智能终端、大数据辅助诊治等医疗运作模式。让人民享受到高科技带来的获得感和幸福感。

李紫恒 摄

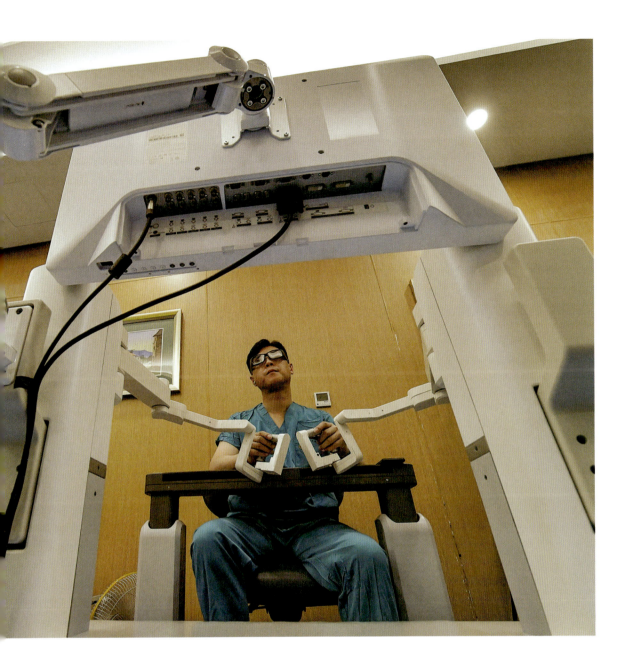

5G-assisted remote surgical operation

In September 2020, the Affiliated Hospital of Qingdao University completes a 5G ultra long-distance urology operation.

At present, the areas attracting most attention in science and technology are AI, cloud computing, 5G, and IoT. In the 5G era, AI can provide faster response, richer content, smarter applications, and better user experience. 5G will not only boost the speed of Internet, but also shore up shortcomings restricting the development of AI and serve as a new driving force for artificial intelligence.

Smart medical care, with the support of 5G, will make medical operation models such as rapid first aid, telemedicine, new health management, smart terminals, and big data-assisted diagnosis and treatment possible, bringing people sense of satisfaction and happiness.

Photo by Li Ziheng

原山林场，艰苦创业成就的绿色海洋

2020 年 10 月 17 日，全国第二处"林业英雄林"正式在淄博原山林场落成，成为中国"林业英雄林"在林业英雄所在林场落成的首例。（见下页图）

原山林场自 1957 年建场以来，几代原山人面对荒山秃岭，艰苦奋斗绿化荒山（见右图），成就了今天原山的绿色海洋。改革开放以来，原山林场积极探索，特别是在全国人大代表、全国林业英雄孙建博的带领下，开创了林场保生态、企业创效益、公园创品牌的"一场两制"改革发展模式，完成了从荒山秃岭到绿水青山，进而到金山银山的美丽嬗变。原山林场的改革创新经验成为中国林业战线的一面旗帜和国有林场改革的样板。

Barren hills turned into lush woods

The photo on the right shows the view of barren hills of Yuanshan in the past, and the photo on the next page shows how the Yuanshan Forestry Area looks today.

On October 17, 2020, the second "Forest for Afforestation Hero" in the country was launched in Zibo Yuanshan Forestry Area, making it the first forest completed in the area where the afforestation hero is located.

Since its establishment in 1957, Yuanshan Forestry Area has been transformed from the barren hills to today's green forest through the strenuous efforts of generations of Yuanshan people. Since the reform and opening-up, Yuanshan has been exploring actively. In particular, under the leadership of Sun Jianbo, a NPC deputy and a national afforestation hero, Yuanshan has created a reform model of "one forest, two systems", in which the environment, revenues and brand are ensured by forest, business and park respectively. The forestry area has realized the transformation from barren hills and wasteland to lush mountains and clear water, and then to valuable assets. The reform and innovation experience of Yuanshan has become a pacesetter for China's afforestation efforts and a model for the reform of state-owned forestry areas.

"万里黄河第一隧"

　　2020年10月，"万里黄河第一隧"施工现场。

　　"万里黄河第一隧"将进一步打通济南主城区与济南新旧动能转换起步区的来往通道。

　　近年来，济南城市规模不断扩展，但南部的群山与北部的黄河，似乎成为济南人心中的"天然"屏障。在"山河之间"，当代济南东西狭长的城市空间，逐渐形成。进入21世纪，济南的城市规划者们越来越意识到，要彻底释放这座城市的发展潜力，济南必须突破南北之界限。2017年底，作为济南携河北跨重要交通支撑的"三桥一隧"项目陆续开工建设，"万里黄河第一隧"正式破土动工。2021年1月23日，"万里黄河第一隧"全线贯通。

郭尧 摄

The first tunnel under the Yellow River

This photo shows the construction site of the first tunnel under the Yellow River in October 2020.

This tunnel will further connect the main urban area of Jinan and the Jinan Start-up Area for Growth Drivers Transformation.

Jinan has been expanding in recent years. However, the mountains in the south and the Yellow River in the north seem to become a natural barrier to the city, hence the formation of Jinan's long and narrow east-to-west urban area. In the 21st century, urban planners in Jinan are increasingly aware that Jinan must break through the boundaries in the north and south in order to fully release the potential of the city. At the end of 2017, 3 bridges and 1 tunnel, which support Jinan's efforts in developing the northern area of the Yellow River, started one after another, and the first tunnel under the Yellow River officially broke ground. On January 23, 2021, the construction of tunnel was completed.

Photo by Guo Yao

曹县的"汉服博士"

2020 年 12 月，在菏泽曹县汉服生产车间里，胡春青和他的妻子正在给主播装饰。

留在大城市奋斗还是回家乡创业？很多人纠结多年都没有答案。在有着"淘宝县"之称的山东曹县，不少年轻人却坚定地选择了后者。

"85 后"胡春青是大连理工大学的一名在读博士生，2018 年底返乡创业时，父亲坚决反对，但在他看来，全镇遍地的淘宝店和动辄上亿的销售额，已经让追求美好生活的方式发生了改变。过去农村人要想过好日子，普遍选择进城打工；而现在，美好生活近在家门口。

回乡半年，胡春青新开店铺的销售额就达到了 500 万元。渐渐地，质疑声没有了，夫妻俩成了曹县年轻人心中的榜样，肩上也多了一份责任和担当。

如今胡春青成了淘宝镇的"明星"，他和妻子一起做原创设计，带领村民提前布局，让"戏服村"转型成了"原创汉服村"。

郭绪雷 摄

Get ready to sell traditional dresses online

In December 2020, Hu Chunqing and his wife dress an anchor up in a Hanfu (a kind of traditional Chinese clothing) production workshop in Caoxian County, Heze City.

Stay in the big city or go back home to start a business? This is a decision that many people have been struggling to make. However, in Caoxian of Shandong Province, the "Taobao County", many young people firmly choose the latter.

Hu Chunqing, born in 1986, is a PhD student at Dalian University of Technology. When he returned to his hometown to start a business at the end of 2018, his father firmly opposed it. But in his opinion, the Taobao shops all over the town, many of which boast sales of hundreds of millions of yuan, have changed the way of pursuing a better life. In the past, people in rural areas generally chose to work in cities if they wanted to live a good life. Now, a good life is on the doorstep.

After returning home for half a year, sales of Hu Chunqing's new store reached 5 million yuan. Gradually, doubts disappeared. The couple became a role model for the young people in Caoxian, and along with it came a greater sense of responsibility.

Now Hu Chunqing has become a star in the Taobao County. He and his wife worked on original designs, led the villagers to make preparations in advance, and transformed the village from producing opera costumes to Hanfu.

Photo by Guo Xulei

牡丹机场，壮志凌云

2021 年 4 月 2 日，菏泽牡丹机场首航。

牡丹机场首批开通西安、上海、厦门等 5 个城市航线，下一步将陆续开通北京、广州、深圳等 16 个城市 10 条航线，千万菏泽人民实现了在家门口坐飞机的"航空梦"。

作为鲁苏豫皖四省交界重要的交通枢纽，牡丹机场通航后将提升菏泽市的综合实力、城市竞争力，有助于菏泽更好地对接京津冀、长三角、粤港澳大湾区等发达区域，深度融入新发展格局，加快打造全省内陆开放新高地。

A new airport opened in Shandong

On April 2, 2021, Heze Mudan Airport makes its maiden flight.

The first batch of air routes is to 5 cities, including Xi'an, Shanghai, and Xiamen. Another 10 air routes to 16 cities, such as Beijing, Guangzhou and Shenzhen, will be opened successively. Tens of millions of Heze people have realized their dream of taking airplanes at their doorstep.

As an important transportation hub at the junction of the four provinces of Shandong, Jiangsu, Henan and Anhui, Heze City will see a boost in its composite strength and competitiveness after the opening of Mudan Airport. Heze will be able to better connect with more developed areas, like Beijing, Tianjin and Hebei, the Yangtze River Delta, as well as the Guangdong-Hong Kong-Macao Greater Bay Area, integrate into the new development paradigm, and step up the efforts of building itself into a pacesetter of opening-up in Shandong's inland areas.

后 记

　　在迎来中国共产党成立 100 周年之际，为真实、生动地记录山东小康工程的建设历程，在中共山东省委宣传部的指导下，山东画报出版社策划出版了这本影像纪实作品——《俺们》。本书中的 100 组照片，是我们献给这个伟大时代的一首首诗歌、一朵朵浪花。

　　小康承载初心，小康属于人民。从这个意义上讲，我们通过选取山东百姓的日常生活图片，从生活变迁的微观视角，用一个个脱贫攻坚的生动案例和致富奔小康的真实故事，记录下山东人民在这一历史进程中的表情和心情、足迹和轨迹。因此，阅览本书，我们希望读者能体味其中的人文性、纪实性、艺术性，在相关文字的表述方面，我们也力图兼顾理性的叙事和感性的抒情。照片中的每一张笑脸，每一个幸福的瞬间，都在感染着本书编写者。我们也盼望这些照片和文字，能走到每位读者的心里。

　　感谢社会各界在本书编辑过程中给予的大力支持。感谢中共山东省委党校（山东行政学院）二级教授杨珍，由她撰写的《小康社会建设历史演进与多维创新》一文作为本书之"综述"，为本书的组织和撰写提供了研究基础和成果支持。感谢中共山东省委党校（山东行政学院）教育长王军，为本书的组织编写提供了支持。感谢谷永威、庞守义、李百军、李霞、曾毅、汤序民、王剑、杨超等摄影家的鼎力相助，他们是山东小康社会进程中的"拾光者"。感谢徐敏、白云、徐文、林彦银、张宝亮、张兴东等诸位朋友和各界人士的撰稿，大家的努力与付出，使得那些照片更加流光溢彩。

本书图片重点定格普通百姓奔小康的奋斗和喜悦瞬间，力图通过一个个鲜活的生命个体在历史中的状态，展示小康社会的发展进程。当然，山东小康建设的历程是很难通过这百多幅照片完全呈现和表达的。难以言尽或纰漏之处，敬请读者见谅。

我们希望每位读者在看到这些图片时，会高兴地说："看，这就是俺们的小康生活！"

2021 年 6 月

Epilog

As we celebrate the centenary of the Communist Party of China, Shandong Pictorial Publishing House published this photo documentary, under the guidance of the Publicity Department of the CPC Shandong Provincial Committee, in a bid to vividly and aptly capture Shandong's experience in building a moderately prosperous society. The 100 photos in the book are poems and flowers we dedicate to this great era.

The building of a moderately prosperous society is for the people, which echoes the original aspiration of the CPC. In this sense, by selecting pictures of the daily life of the people in Shandong and with vivid cases of poverty alleviation and the stories of living a better-off life, we have recorded people's experience and life trajectories from a microscopic perspective of changes in life. It is our hope that readers can appreciate its humanity, authenticity, and artistry, and our efforts in balancing rational narration and emotional expression. As editors, we are deeply moved by every smile in the photos and every moment of happiness in this book, and we hope our readers could feel the same.

Thanks to various sectors of society for the strong support in editing this book. Thanks to Yang Zhen, a level 2 professor of the Party School of the CPC Shandong Provincial Committee (Shandong Academy of Governance). Her article *"Historical Evolution and Multi-dimensional Innovation in the Building of a Moderately Prosperous Society"* serves as the "overview" of this book, providing research foundation and support for the book. Thanks to Wang Jun, Chief Education Director of the Party School of the CPC Shandong Provincial Committee (Shandong Academy of Governance), for supporting the editing and compiling work. Thanks to Gu Yongwei, Pang Shouyi, Li Baijun, Li Xia, Zeng Yi, Tang Xumin, Wang Jian, Yang Chao and other photographers for their help. They are the "moment collectors" in the process of building a moderately prosperous society in Shandong. Thanks to Xu Min, Bai Yun, Xu Wen, Lin Yanyin, Zhang Baoliang, Zhang Xingdong and other friends and people from all walks of life for their contributions. It is all these people's hard work and dedication that have made the photos more brilliant.

The photos focus on the moments of struggle and joy of ordinary people on the path toward a moderately prosperous society. That said, it is almost impossible to fully present the process of building such a society with only 100 photos. We hope the readers could understand if there are any omissions or mistakes.

We also hope that when our readers see these pictures, they will say, "Look, this is the journey we have taken to a moderately prosperous life."

June 2021

图书在版编目（CIP）数据

俺们：山东小康之路影像纪实：汉英对照／本书编写组编；
山东省外事翻译中心译. --济南：山东画报出版社，2021.10
　　ISBN 978-7-5474-3769-8

Ⅰ.①俺… Ⅱ.①本… Ⅲ.①小康建设—山东—摄影集
Ⅳ.①F127.52-64

中国版本图书馆CIP数据核字（2021）第197433号

俺们：山东小康之路影像纪实

Our Good Times: A Collection of Photos of Shandong's Journey to General Prosperity

本书编写组 编
Edited by the Editing Group
山东省省外事翻译中心 译
Translated by Shandong Provincial Translation and Interpretation Center

责任编辑　赵祥斌　陈先云　张　欢　王伟辰　孙程程
Responsible Editors: Zhao Xiangbin　Chen Xianyun　Zhang Huan
　　　　　　　　　　 Wang Weichen　Sun Chengcheng
特邀编辑　杨立龙
Guest Editor: Yang Lilong
装帧设计　王　芳
Graphic Designer: Wang Fang

出 版 人　李文波
主管单位　山东出版传媒股份有限公司
出版发行　山东画报出版社
　　　　　社　　　址　济南市市中区英雄山路189号B座　邮编 250002
　　　　　电　　　话　总编室（0531）82098472
　　　　　　　　　　　市场部（0531）82098479　82098476（传真）
　　　　　网　　　址　http：//www.hbcbs.com.cn
　　　　　电子信箱　hbcb@sdpress.com.cn
印　　刷　山东临沂新华印刷物流集团有限责任公司
规　　格　185毫米×260毫米　1/16
　　　　　17印张　106幅图　80千字
版　　次　2021年10月第1版
印　　次　2021年10月第1次印刷
书　　号　ISBN 978-7-5474-3769-8
定　　价　168.00元

如有印装质量问题，请与出版社总编室联系更换。